T2-EYK-208

YOUR RIGHTS WHEN YOU OWE TOO MUCH

Gudrun M. Nickel
Attorney at Law

SPHINX® PUBLISHING
AN IMPRINT OF SOURCEBOOKS, INC.®
NAPERVILLE, ILLINOIS

This book was formerly titled *Debtors' Rights*. We have updated or changed the sample forms, statutes, and information in addition to changing the title to ensure that it is the most current at the time of publication.

First Edition, 2001

Published by: **Sphinx® Publishing, An Imprint of Sourcebooks, Inc.®**

Naperville Office
P.O. Box 4410
Naperville, Illinois 60567-4410
630-961-3900
Fax: 630-961-2168
http://www.sourcebooks.com

This publication is designed to provide accurate and authoritative information in regard to the subject matter covered. It is sold with the understanding that the publisher is not engaged in rendering legal, accounting, or other professional service. If legal advice or other expert assistance is required, the services of a competent professional person should be sought.

From a Declaration of Principles Jointly Adopted by a Committee of the American Bar Association and a Committee of Publishers and Associations

This product is not a substitute for legal advice.

Disclaimer required by Texas statutes.

Library of Congress Cataloging-in-Publication Data
Nickel, Gudrun M.
      Your rights when you owe too much / Gudrun M. Nickel.
          p. cm. -- (Legal survival guides)
      Rev. ed. of: Debtors' rights. 3rd ed. 1998.
      Includes index.
      ISBN 1-57248-157-9
      1. Debtor and creditor--United States--Popular works. 2. Actions and defenses--United States--Popular works. 3. Bankruptcy--United States--Popular works. I. Nickel, Gudrun M. Debtors' rights. II. Title. III. Series.

KF1539.Z9 N534 2001
346.7307'7--dc21   2001041172

Printed and bound in the United States of America.
BG Paperback — 10 9 8 7 6 5 4 3 2 1

CONTENTS

Acknowledgment

To my husband, Bob Robinson, for his invaluable contribution

USING SELF-HELP
LAW BOOKS

Before using a self-help law book, you should realize the advantages and disadvantages of doing your own legal work and understand the challenges and diligence that this requires.

Rest assured that you won't be the first or only person handling your own legal matter. For example, in some states, more than seventy-five percent of divorces and other cases have at least one party representing him or herself. Because of the high cost of legal services, this is a major trend and many courts are struggling to make it easier for people to represent themselves. However, some courts are not happy with people who do not use attorneys and refuse to help them in any way. For some, the attitude is, "Go to the law library and figure it out for yourself."

We at Sphinx write and publish self-help law books to give people an alternative to the often complicated and confusing legal books found in most law libraries. We have made the explanations of the law as simple and easy to understand as possible. Of course, unlike an attorney advising an individual client, we cannot cover every conceivable possibility.

Whenever you shop for a product or service, you are faced with various levels of quality and price. In deciding what product or service to buy, you make a cost/value analysis on the basis of your willingness to pay and the quality you desire.

When buying a car, you decide whether you want transportation, comfort, status, or sex appeal. Accordingly, you decide among such choices as a Neon, a Lincoln, a Rolls Royce, or a Porsche. Before making a decision, you usually weigh the merits of each option against the cost.

When you get a headache, you can take a pain reliever (such as aspirin) or visit a medical specialist for a neurological examination. Given this choice, most people, of course, take a pain reliever, since it costs only pennies; whereas a medical examination costs hundreds of dollars and takes a lot of time. This is usually a logical choice because it is rare to need anything more than a pain reliever for a headache. But in some cases, a headache may indicate a brain tumor and failing to see a specialist right away can result in complications. Should everyone with a headache go to a specialist? Of course not, but people treating their own illnesses must realize that they are betting on the basis of their cost/value analysis of the situation. They are taking the most logical option.

The same cost/value analysis must be made when deciding to do one's own legal work. Many legal situations are very straight forward, requiring a simple form and no complicated analysis. Anyone with a little intelligence and a book of instructions can handle the matter without outside help.

But there is always the chance that complications are involved that only an attorney would notice. To simplify the law into a book like this, several legal cases often must be condensed into a single sentence or paragraph. Otherwise, the book would be several hundred pages long and too complicated for most people. However, this simplification necessarily leaves out many details and nuances that would apply to special or unusual situations. Also, there are many ways to interpret most legal questions. Your case may come before a judge who disagrees with the analysis of our authors.

Therefore, in deciding to use a self-help law book and to do your own legal work, you must realize that you are making a cost/value analysis. You have decided that the money you will save in doing it yourself outweighs the chance that your case will not turn out to your satisfaction. Most people handling their own simple legal matters never have a problem, but occasionally people find that it ended up costing them more to have an attorney straighten out the situation than it would have if they had hired an attorney in the beginning. Keep this in mind if you decide to handle your own case, and be sure to consult an attorney if you feel you might need further guidance.

The next thing to remember is that a book which covers the law for the entire nation, or even for an entire state, cannot possibly include every procedural difference of every county court. In some cases, each state or county, or even each judge, may require unique forms and procedures. In our *state* books, our forms usually cover the majority of counties in the state, or provide examples of the type of form that will be required. In our *national* books, our forms are sometimes even more general in nature but are designed to give a good idea of the type of form that will be needed in most locations. Nonetheless, keep in mind that your *state*, county, or judge may have a requirement, or use a form, that is not included in this book.

You should not necessarily expect to be able to get all of the information and resources you need solely from within the pages of this book. This book will serve as your guide, giving you specific information whenever possible and helping you to find out what else you will need to know. This is just like if you decided to build your own backyard deck. You might purchase a book on how to build decks. However, such a book would not include the building codes and permit requirements of every city, town, county, and township in the nation; nor would it include the lumber, nails, saws, hammers, and other materials and tools you would need to actually build the deck. You would use the book as your guide, and then do some work and research involving such matters as whether you need a permit of some kind, what type and grade of wood are available in your area, whether to use hand tools or power tools, and how to use those tools.

Besides being subject to state and local rules and practices, the law is subject to change at any time. The courts and the legislatures of all fifty states are constantly revising the laws. It is possible that while you are reading this book, some aspect of the law is being changed or that a court is interpreting a law in a different way. You should always check the most recent statutes, rules and regulations to see what, if any, changes have been made.

In most cases, the change will be of minimal significance. A form will be redesigned, additional information will be required, or a waiting period will be extended. As a result, you might need to revise a form, file an extra form, or wait out a longer time period; these types of changes will not usually affect the outcome of your case. On the other hand, sometimes a major part of the law is changed, the entire law in a particular area is rewritten, or a case that was the basis of a central legal point is overruled. In such instances, your entire ability to pursue your case may be impaired.

Again, you should weigh the value of your case against the cost of an attorney and make a decision as to what you believe is in your best interest.

INTRODUCTION

After a period of unprecedented economic growth in the United States, employers are beginning to layoff workers. The technology and manufacturing industries are often in the news, reporting job cuts in record numbers. These layoffs come at a time when consumers owe more money, have less equity in their properties, and are saving less than at any time in the past 20 years. For many the economic boom may become a bust. Bankruptcy filings in the first quarter of 2001 were up over 15 per cent from the same period in 2000.

Although careless spending—particularly purchases on credit—is likely to result in unwanted consequences, even the most responsible and conscientious person can experience a change in economic circumstances that may be financially and psychologically devastating. Lifetime careers sometimes die an early death; if you become ill, there is often too little or no disability insurance. A job loss or illness can make it difficult, if not impossible, to meet your financial obligations. Lenders who were once pursuing you to lend you money will soon pursue you to get the money back if you fail to make the required payments.

The only way to avoid having creditors is to avoid having any debt. However, most people have a mortgage on their homes, have purchased one or several vehicles on credit, may have a consumer loan for household items, and have a number of credit cards. Your creditors—mortgage and finance companies, banks, credit card companies, etc.—all expect to get paid.

When you do not pay, your creditor has a number of options available in attempting to collect an outstanding debt. The creditor can:

- send your account to a collection agency. The agency rather than the creditor will then write and call you to try to collect the payment. (If the creditor *assigns* its right to the account, the collection agency can sue for the amount due in its own name.);

- report your unpaid bill directly to a credit reporting service (credit bureau), and then send it to a *collection agency;*

- get a *judgment* against you in court;

- *foreclose* on your real estate and get a *deficiency* judgment if the sale proceeds are not enough to cover the debt;

- repossess your *personal property* that is used as security for a loan, sell it, and get a deficiency judgment if the amount of the sale is not enough to cover the debt;

- get an assignment of property you are expecting to receive, such as a tax return or royalties;

- take your property, either before or after getting a judgment against you;

- garnish your wages; or
- force you into bankruptcy.

Although most people do not openly discuss financial problems, they are a reality of life, particularly in an economy where thousands of people are being laid-off or terminated from their jobs. Even if you are getting unemployment benefits, they may not be sufficient to meet the financial obligations you took on while earning a good wage or salary.

It is easy to become overwhelmed by the pressure of collectors' calls and a mailbox full of overdue bills. Being served with a summons in a lawsuit filed by a creditor to collect an unpaid debt—a good possibility if your bills are overdue—is an experience most people would rather live without.

Becoming overwhelmed or having anxiety attacks does not solve financial problems. In order to deal with financial setbacks effectively, it is important to have an understanding of what your rights are, the extent a creditor can actually go in collecting a debt, and how you can defend yourself against the actions your creditors might take to collect debts.

This book will explain what types of actions creditors can take against you for non-payment and your possible defenses to those actions.

The federal laws apply if:

- you enter into a written agreement with the creditor regarding the debt;
- the extension of credit is for personal, family, or household purposes;

- if the creditor (or collector) involved, during the immediately preceding calendar year, entered into agreements with consumers involving interest or finance charges, or extensions of credit involving more than four installments more than twenty-five times; and

- payments are to be made in more than four installments or interest is added which was not previously charged.

This book contains information about your rights under these federal laws regarding collection agencies, credit reporting, consumer loans, credit cards, and leases in Chapters 4, 5, 8, and 9.

An isolated transaction with someone to whom you owe money will probably not be regulated by federal law; however, there may be state laws for your protection. Chapters 12 and 13 deal with judgments and collections and they will apply whether or not your loan or lease transaction is subject to federal law.

In a good economy, lenders readily give credit to most people—many lenders even have employees whose sole job is to find borrowers. In some cases, perhaps lenders were overly zealous in their efforts to extend credit to you, and now when times are tough, you may find it difficult to repay those obligations. There are numerous laws that have been enacted to protect borrowers from certain lender and creditor tactics, and you may find that you indeed have some recourse by reading this entire book.

Having a better understanding of the different types of debt you have incurred, and what your legal rights are in the event of your inability to repay a loan or credit obligation, will help you take control of whatever financial dilemma you may find. You should take some comfort in knowing that you can no longer be put into prison for being in debt based upon any type of contractual obligation to pay. (Rhode Island statute Chapter 10-13 provides that a debtor must be released from prison after swearing to the judge that he has no money or property with which to pay the debt.)

Being in overwhelming debt should be viewed as a temporary condition—in which you may find yourself due to present circumstances. It is a condition that can be changed, through your own efforts in dealing with creditors or perhaps ultimately filing a bankruptcy petition.

Chapter 14 will give you bankruptcy information. The most important point to keep in mind is that all hope is not lost. Chapter 17 will help you better protect yourself from financial problems in the future.

Some chapters include a section on how to exercise your rights or defenses with some sample letters and forms. You should use these with other resources available to you, including your local law library (often your local library will have books that contain your state as well as federal laws), your state or district attorney's office, your local court clerk, and your state or local consumer affairs or public service office. The state offices are listed at the back of this book as Appendix B.

There may be a Government Printing Office bookstore in your area that has publications available regarding the federal Truth-in-Lending disclosure requirements, the Fair Credit

Billing Act, the Consumer Credit Reporting Reform Act of
1996, the Fair Credit Leasing Act, and other information. (See
Appendix A.) For your convenience and for further research,
the sources of information are listed at the end of each chapter. Information about credit and your rights as a consumer is
available from:

Federal Consumer Information Center
Pueblo, Colorado 81009
800-668-9889
http://www.pueblo.gsa.gov/

You will find that the terms *lender* and *creditor* are used repeatedly. Although there may be a technical difference in that a
lender is in the business of lending money, while a creditor is
in the business of extending credit (such as a credit card company), the terms are used interchangeably.

FREQUENTLY ASKED QUESTIONS 1

Mortgages, car loans, credit card payments, medical and dental bills, can become overwhelming and result in problems far beyond the immediate financial ones. The most frequently asked questions regarding debt, bill collectors, credit bureaus, the IRS, bankruptcy follow. Remember, all of these issues are covered in greater detail in the text. Frequent reference will be made in the book to creditor and debtor. The *creditor* is an individual or company to whom you owe money—it can be a bank, credit card company, bank, savings and loan, or your doctor. A *debtor* refers to the person who owes the money to the creditor.

Question: How will I know when I am in financial trouble?

***Answer*:** There are several signs that you may need help with your finances, including:

- juggling your bills from paycheck to paycheck, and not being able to pay them all at one time;

- getting late payment reminders in the mail from your creditors;

- getting telephone calls from bill collectors. (This usually means that the person or company you originally owed money to has given up trying to collect the debt and has turned the account over to a collection agency.)

Remember, most people in this country are in debt--debt includes the mortgage on your house, car and boat loans, loans to buy appliances and furniture, as well as medical and other bills.

Question: How do people get into financial trouble?

Answer: Of course we have all heard the story about the family who accepts every credit card that is offered by mail, then charges each card up to the maximum limit and cannot make the payments. Or, they can make just the bare minimum payment, which means that the outstanding balance, with accrued interest, may take an eternity to pay off. This problem stems in part from irresponsible use of credit, as well as eager credit card companies.

However, there are also many people who suffer catastrophies for which they simply are not prepared. For example, a medical emergency without proper insurance, or a job lay-off, can have serious financial consequences for a family, and financial troubles often lead to other problems.

Question: Do I really have legal rights if I owe money?

Answer: Many people are surprised that there are laws, both state and federal, which protect them. For example, federal laws under the Consumer Credit Act include the Fair Debt Collection Practices Act, which protects you from being threatened by collection agency employees. Also under the Consumer Credit Act, the Fair Credit Reporting Act regulates credit reporting agencies and allows you to file a complaint with the government.

There are laws requiring auto leasing companies to give you certain information before you sign loan documents, laws requiring auto leasing companies to give you certain information about the lease, and laws giving you an opportunity to tell your side of story if the bank wants to foreclose your mortgage and take your house. If you find that bankruptcy is your only option, laws will allow you to keep certain property.

Of course, in order to use these laws to your advantage, you must know how they protect you, and what action you need to take to protect yourself.

Question: What can we do to prepare for an expected loss of income which will make it difficult, if not impossible to pay bills?

Answer: The first step is to notify all your creditors that you are having financial difficulties, and in some cases it may help to explain why. Ask the creditors if they will work with you on a reduced payment plan, perhaps giving you a few months of "breathing room". Ask your home mortgage company if you could make interest-only payments for a period of time (provided these payments would be substantially less than the total), or a reduced payment with any unpaid interest to be added to the later payments after you get back on stronger financial feet. Be sure to ask your creditors if they will agree not to report your reduced payments to the credit bureau, as long as you keep your part of the agreement.

Consider selling some of your assets to pay your bills. For example, sell your new car and buy an older, used model which would not only reduce or eliminate your payments, but should also reduce your insurance premium.

Question: I have a mortgage on my house, car payments, payments on some living room furniture, and several credit card bills. Is there a difference between these loans?

Answer: The mortgage on your house and the loan on your car are probably *secured debts*. In other words, the bank or creditors which loaned you the money to buy the house and the car have a legal interest in that property, which is referred to as *collateral*. If you do not pay, they have the right to take your property. This usually involves a court proceeding. The bank or the creditor will then sell the property to get its money, and in most states can ask you to pay the difference between what the bank received from the sale and what was actually owed. This is called a *deficiency*.

The other type of loan is *unsecured*. This means that the creditor has no collateral. However, the creditor can still sue in court, get a judgment against you, and then try to take your property, or take the money from your paycheck, to pay the debt. What property a creditor can take, and how it can be taken, varies from state to state.

Question: What if my ex-spouse and I agree to split the debts, and my ex-spouse refuses to pay? A hospital where he (or she) had some surgery done keeps sending me threatening letters, but he (or she) agreed to pay the bill!

Answer: Unless the creditor, in this case the hospital, agrees in writing that it will look only to your ex-spouse for payment, your original agreement with the creditor still stands. In other words, the hospital is not a party to the agreement between you and your ex-spouse. If your ex-spouse does not pay, that leaves you responsible! You can sue your ex-spouse for not living up to his or her part of the agreement.

Question: Is it not true that if I make a payment of $1.00 per month on a bill, I cannot be sued by the creditor?

Answer: This is a misconception that is absolutely wrong. If you owe an individual or a company money, that creditor has the right to get paid in the full amount that is due, unless of course there is a valid legal defense to the bill. The *defenses*, that is, your possible legal and acceptable reasons for a non-payment, are explained in detail in the book. However making a payment of $1.00 per month is not a valid defense.

Question: What is a credit bureau, or *credit reporting agency*

Answer: A credit bureau or *credit reporting agency* is a service that provides prospective creditors with the information about you, primarily the debts that you have, your payment record, and loan to buy a house, the bank will request a credit report. This report will tell the bank how many credit cards and other loans you have, whether or not you make your payments on time, whether someone has sued you and obtained a money judgment, and whether you have filed bankruptcy within the last 7 years. There are three major credit reporting agencies in the country, namely Equifax, Experian, and TransUnion.

Question: If a creditor reports my late payments to a credit bureau, even though I am doing the best that I can, what should I do?

Answer: You usually find out that a creditor has reported this type of information when you apply for a loan. If you are turned down for the loan because of your credit report, you have a right to a copy of the report free of charge. Otherwise, you can request a copy of your report from any of the credit bureaus, typically for a small fee. If there are negative notations on the report, write a letter to the credit bureau explaining the reason for the late or lower payments, and ask that a copy be given to anyone who requests a report. Before you apply for credit, you should make the prospective creditor aware of your situation so that there are no surprises for either the creditor or you.

Question: What can I do if information on my credit report is wrong, for example, if there is an unpaid doctor bill on the report, to a doctor I do not even know? (Or if a bank loan that was paid off six months ago shows up as unpaid?)

Answer: The first step is to notify the credit reporting service, in writing, of the error. Be sure to send all letters certified, with a return receipt requested. If you are not sure how this is done, take your letter to the post office and tell the clerk that you want the addressee to sign a receipt for the letter. The clerk will give you the forms to complete. Once you have the receipt, the credit reporting service cannot claim that it did not receive your letter.

The letter should clearly state which entry in the report is incorrect, and why. The reporting agency must investigate, and correct the report if the information is found to be inaccurate. If the agency does not do what is required by law, you can file a complaint with the Federal Trade Commission.

Question: If all of my efforts to negotiate a reduced payment plan with a creditor fail, and the creditor does get a court judgment against me, how long will it stay on my record?

Answer: The credit report agencies will keep the judgment on your report for a period of seven years, unless the law in your state allows for a longer period of time, or the law allows the creditor to periodically renew the judgment. In some states the judgment can stay on your report for as long as 21 years. This may make it difficult for you to buy a house or make other purchases on credit in the future.

Question: I have been receiving a lot of advertisements from companies promising to repair my bad credit. Are these legitimate?

Answer: You cannot change your credit history; no amount of money paid to a credit repair company will eliminate the fact that you owe money, or failed to make payments in the past. The best "credit fix" is a disciplined budget and an effort to negotiate with and payoff your outstanding debts. The "credit repair" service, which will undoubtedly charge you a fee, may become another creditor.

Question: Several months ago I was having difficulty paying some of my bills because my hours at work were cut back, and I received letters from a collection agency threatening me with a lawsuit if I did not pay. Can you explain what a collection agency is?

Answer: A *collection agency* is a business that earns money by collecting debts for other people. For example, if you owe money to a doctor bill, and you are unable to work a payment plan directly with the doctors office, that doctor's office might turn the bill over to a collection agency. The collection agency usually gets a percentage of the amount it collects, and the balance goes to the creditor.

Question: Is there anything I can do to keep the debt collectors from calling at odd hours to collect a payment that I do not feel I owe?

Answer: The Fair Debt Collection Practices Act clearly states during what hours a collector may call you (8 am to 9 pm). You should first tell the collector that your are aware of your rights under the Act, and that you will file a complaint with the Federal Trade Commission if he or she does not stop. As soon as you receive your written notice from the collector, you should respond by certified mail, return receipt requested, explaining why you dispute the debt. The collector should not contact you again, but may pursue whatever legal remedies are available to collect payment. If a lawsuit is filed, you may then give your side of the story to the court. (You might also attempt contacting the creditor directly.)

Question: Even though I have a fixed income, I get applications for credit cards in the mail—what should I do with them?

Answer: First, decide whether it is important or necessary that you have a credit card, and ask yourself whether you will use it responsibly. If the answers are yes to both questions, then:

- check the interest rate the credit card company is charging, whether it is only an introductory low rate, or if it will go up—compare the rate with other companies;

- be sure you understand the repayment terms, whether you can pay the balance in monthly payments, or whether the entire balance must be paid off monthly (for example—at most—American Express cards require the entire balance be paid in full every month); and

- check whether you will be charged a yearly fee to use this card—try to find a credit card company that does not charge a yearly fee.

Question: A good friend is having a difficult time buying a car because in the past he was late on a few bills—which shows up on his credit report—and now cannot qualify for a loan. His banker told him that the bank would give him a loan if he has a co-signer. My friend than asked me if would co-sign his loan for him. Can you explain what this means to me?

Answer: Being a co-signer on a loan makes you as responsible for repayment as your friend. If your friend does not make the payments, or is late for any reason, the bank can immediately try to get the money from you. Parents often co-sign for loans for their children, since the children usually have not established a good credit report by the time they get their first car. In your case , however, you probably will not have as much control over whether your friend honors his obligation to the bank as most parents have over their children. Also remember that, if your friend defaults and you are unable to pay the bank back, your credit report will also suffer.

Question: I am thinking about going into business for myself, and will need to rent office space and lease some office equipment. Although I have already formed a company, the landlord and the leasing service insist that I *personally guarantee* the rental agreement. I thought that if I have a company, only the company should sign—is this not correct?

Answer: The landlord and equipment leasing company want to make sure that they get their money, even if your business fails. Your *personal guarantee* gives them the right to hold you personally responsible if your company cannot pay its bills. When you are personally responsible for the payments, your personal property, except of course that property that is exempt from creditors as explained in the book, can be taken by the landlord or the leasing company. Usually this requires that the landlord or equipment leasing company go to court and get a judgment against you first.

Question: Please describe how a creditor can take my property if I have not given the creditor a security interest as you explained earlier.

Answer: This is more easily explained by example. If you owe any money and do not make the payment when it is due, the person or company to whom you the money can file a lawsuit against you in court. If the judge decides against you, a *judgment* will be entered in the court records. The creditor can then take the next step and ask the court to *attach* (or take) certain items of your property in payment of the debt. If the court agrees, than the sheriff will be given the authority to take the property, sell it, use the money from the sale to pay the creditor, and any remaining amount will be paid to you.

Question: What does it mean to have your wages garnished?

Answer: This is a legal term which means that, after a creditor gets a judgment against you as just described, the creditor can then ask the court to issue a *garnishment*. In other words, a court order will be sent to your employer, demanding that a certain portion of your paycheck be withheld from you and sent

directly to the court for payment t
Every time your paycheck is garnish
getting a smaller amount than usual,
itor will be getting a portion of the money you owe.

The book lists the garnishment laws state by state. Some states do not allow garnishment of wages if you are head of the household, and most put a maximum limit on how much a creditor can get from each paycheck.

Question: I have heard about mortgage foreclosures, but I am not sure how they work. Is this something only bank's can do?

Answer: When you give a lender—regardless of whether the lender is a bank, the previous owner of the property, or your father—a security interest in your property (property here is real estate such as land, a house, or condominium), the lender has a right to take the property if you do not make the payments. Sometimes it is difficult for various reasons to get money from a bank to buy a house, so we get what is known as *seller-financing.* This means that a portion of the purchase price (for example— $75,000.00 of a $100,000.00 house) is financed by the seller. The seller becomes your bank, and will require that his interest in your property be recorded in the appropriate record books. When the payments are not made, your lender has the right to *foreclose* (take your property, have it sold to the highest bidder, get its money back, give you what is left.)

The process is usually easier than that described earlier where a creditor must first get a judgment, then go back to court and ask that the sheriff be allowed to take your property. In the case of a mortgage, the lender already has a right to your property.

Some states use a Trust Deed rather than a mortgage. The procedure is simpler and in some cases does not require a court order.

If your lender is threatening to foreclose its mortgage and take your property, be sure to read your mortgage very carefully to see if the lender is required to drop the foreclosure if you can come up with all the back payments due.

If it is impossible for you to make the outstanding payments, try to negotiate with the lender to take a *deed in lieu of foreclosure*. You would be transferring your ownership to the lender and avoiding the court procedure, and possibly another negative entry on your credit report. Another option is to sell the property as quickly as possible, perhaps at a reduced price, and pay off the lender immediately to avoid court or foreclosure proceedings.

Question: The bank that gave us the money to buy our house required that we sign a stack of papers at closing, some of which I did not even have time to read or understand. Are there laws that protect people like me?

Answer: The Consumer Credit Act specifically requires that creditors provide you with certain information BEFORE you sign up for a loan so that you know exactly what your obligations will be, how much your payments will be, and the total amount the loan will cost you. If you have a 30 year mortgage, you should know how much you will pay the bank if you make each and every payment for 30 years. The bank should also let you know what your closing costs will be. Often there are so-called *points*, an *origination fee*, and other expenses that you will be required to pay for the privilege of borrowing money. These amounts must all be disclosed to you BEFORE you sign and commit yourself to the loan.

Question: I've heard bankruptcy referred to as a "quick fix" for credit problems. Is bankruptcy really a way out of debt?

Answer: Bankruptcy should be used only as a last resort. For example, someone who has only one debt that cannot be paid in time should consider alternatives, such as working out a more reasonable repayment plan with the creditor, selling something to pay the debt, trying to negotiate a lower amount, or temporarily taking on a second job. Although bankruptcy may seem like an easy solution, remember that it will stay on your credit record for at least 7

years and in the meantime you may find it
extremely difficult, if not impossible, to get a mortgage or buy a new car. If a major catastrophe really
does strike within that 7 year period, you will not
be able to file for bankruptcy again.

Another option to regular bankruptcy is a *wage
earners* plan, which requires that you pay each of
your creditors back over a period of time at a
reduced amount. The plan must be approved by
the bankruptcy court. A better option may be consumer credit counseling (such as offered by
Consumer Credit Counseling Services). This a
national organization that provides financial counseling to people with debt problems. A counselor
will work with you and your creditors to come up
with a repayment plan.

NOTE: *A new bankruptcy law, which may make it
difficult to eliminate certain debts, is currently under
consideration in the U.S. Congress.*

Question: If I do file bankruptcy, is there any property I can
keep for myself, or must all of my property be sold
to pay my creditors?

Answer: Certain property is considered exempt from bankruptcy. In most cases you may keep your home (up
to a specific dollar value) and some items of personal property. The types and value of property that
is exempt are listed in this book, in Chapter 14.

Question: Will I still owe money after I file for bankruptcy, or will bankruptcy wipe out all of my debts so that I can make a fresh start?

Answer: It depends upon the debt. If you went on a major shopping spree, or took a luxury vacation, and spent thousands of dollars using your credit cards, your creditors may convince the bankruptcy court that you should not be released from your obligation to repay the money. Bankruptcy will not eliminate most tax obligations (due for the three years immediately before filing), particularly not social security, or withholding payments you as an employer should have made for your employees.

Also, bankruptcy will not eliminate child support and alimony obligations.

Question: Finally, we have often heard the phrase "don't mess with the IRS". Is there anything that can be done if I owe the IRS money?

Answer: First, do not assume that the IRS is always correct. However, always respond to any IRS notice within the time allowed, to avoid any additional penalties and interest over and above the taxes you may owe. Be sure to keep all records—including copies of checks, receipts, and invoices—in case you are audited. The normal time limitations for an audit is 3 years, provided there was no fraud or gross misrepresentation of income. If you disagree with an IRS decision you can file a petition in the U.S. Tax Court. The IRS can take virtually all of your property for taxes

owed—a list of what the IRS cannot take is on page
79 of the book. If you have a serious problem or are
in a crisis situation—such as job loss or medical emergency—the Taxpayer's Bill of Rights does require
that an IRS officer—a Problem Resolution Officer—
work with you to resolve the crisis.

NOTE: *Debt management is not impossible if you have the tools.*

TYPES OF DEBT— AN OVERVIEW 2

SECURED DEBT

All debts are either secured or unsecured. When an interest in property is given to your lender to make the loan safe, you have a *secured* debt. Examples of secured debt are your home mortgage and your car loan. The lender puts everyone on notice about its interest in your property by filing a mortgage on your real estate or a *security* interest in your personal property in the appropriate county or state records. The lender will secure its interest in a car or mobile home by placing its lien directly on the title.

Where the lender has taken the proper steps to record its interest, you cannot sell the property without either paying off the lender or having the buyer take the property subject to the lender's interest. The property given as security is also referred to as *collateral*.

The lender may also take an interest in personal property by taking possession of it.

Example: If you have given the lender stocks and bonds as collateral for your loan, the lender may hold these until the loan is paid off, prohibiting you from using the same stocks and bonds as collateral for other loans or selling them.

Unsecured Debt Becoming Secured Debt

An unsecured debt may become a secured debt if a judgment becomes a *lien* (or claim) on your property. Even without judgments, some states allow liens to be filed. In Florida, for example, condominium associations generally have the right, without first getting a judgment, to place a lien on your property if you do not pay your condominium association assessments. Likewise, people that you employ to work on your property or provide material may be able to file a lien before getting a judgment if you do not pay them.

A *judgment* may also become a lien on your property. Ultimately, the lienholder may take the property and foreclose its lien, just like a creditor to whom you actually gave a security interest in your property. (See Chapters 10 and 11.)

Selling Secured Property

If liens are not paid when you sell your property, they are not removed even if you transfer title. You may have considered selling to get out from under a *mortgage* obligation. However, a sale of property given as security will not necessarily relieve you of your responsibility to pay the mortgage holder, unless he or she agrees to let you off the hook and let your buyer take over the payments. (See Chapter 10.)

If you do not make the loan payments, the lender may, by proper legal proceedings and as specifically spelled out in the loan documents, take the property you have given as collateral. If the other lienholders are not paid when you sell, they can *foreclose* against you and the new title holder. (As for stocks, bonds, and items that the lender can hold in its possession, the lender can then sell them to pay off the debt.)

Lender Selling the Collateral

After the lender sells the collateral, depending upon your loan agreement, he or she will then apply the money from the sale, less expenses, to your loan. This does not necessarily mean that you are no longer liable to your lender. The loan document you signed may also give the lender the right to get a *deficiency judgment* against you if the amount realized from the sale is not enough to pay the balance due on the loan. Deficiency judgments are also discussed in other chapters in this book.

Right of Set-Off

If you have several accounts at one bank as well as a loan, and you fail to make your payments on the loan, the lender may have the right to take the money from your deposit accounts and apply it to your debt. This is called the bank's *right of set-off.*

However, the bank may do this only if this was disclosed to you in the loan documents. The bank cannot use your other accounts as collateral without meeting the disclosure requirement. Otherwise, you can sue the bank for damages, including any cost to you for overdrawn checks. (See Chapter 7.) If the bank has issued you a credit card, it is prohibited from taking funds from other accounts to pay any outstanding amount on the card. (See Chapter 7.)

Bank's Tools

Bad debt has been a problem for banks for a long time. When a customer failed to make a payment within fifteen days of the due date, a late payment letter was sent. The letter was then followed up by a telephone call if no payment was received within thirty days of the due date.

With updated technology, however, a bank or lender can now target individual customers with tailor-made collection techniques. The customer's personal information is reviewed, along with credit reports and other financial information. The combination of information allows the bank or lender to plan its collection efforts on an individual basis. The information also helps the bank or lender decide whether to assign a case to a collection agency, and even suggests how the collection agency should handle the case.

New computer software helps lenders predict which cases are likely to end in repossession of the property, and puts the lender on notice to act immediately when a payment is late.

UNSECURED DEBT

An *unsecured* loan is one for which the lender has taken no collateral. Most credit cards and any loan given to you requiring only your signature are *unsecured loans*. (The signature of someone guaranteeing payment, or a co-signer, is given as security for the debt.) Unsecured debt also includes any amount you owe for services, such as doctor's bills. The service provider (i.e. hospital, doctor, dentist, accountant) and the creditor of an unsecured debt will often first try to contact you personally in an attempt to work out payment of the out-standing bill.

DEBT AFTER A DIVORCE

Marriage, divorce and debt are discussed in detail in Chapter 14. Anyone who is contemplating separation or divorce should keep in mind that an agreement between you and your spouse is effective only between the two of you. Unless a creditor agrees in writing to release one or the other, both parties remain fully responsible for payment.

CONTINGENT LIABILITIES

If you have a *contingent liability*, you will be liable for payment to a creditor only in the event the primary borrower does not pay.

Example: If you have personally guaranteed payment of a business loan and the business can no longer make the payments, the creditor will look to you for the balance owed. Likewise, if you co-sign on a loan for your daughter to buy a car, and she stops making the payments, the lender will come to you. You may be held responsible and pursued by the creditor as with any other debt.

BUSINESS DEBT

If you own your business and the business is having financial difficulties, these difficulties may affect your personal financial situation as well.

Proprietorship or Partnership

As a new business, you may have entered into leases for space and other legal contracts. If operating as a sole proprietorship, you will be held personally responsible for any contract or agreement you enter into. Likewise, signing as a partner does not protect you from personal liability; all partners are usually responsible for partnership debt.

Corporation

You may have set up your business as a corporation, which is considered a separate, legal entity. Although a corporation usually shields its stockholders-owners from liability, you may still have personal liability as an officer or director.

Example: While you may have assumed that setting up your new business as a corporation would relieve you of personal responsibility, your creditors and landlords probably required that you sign "personally," or that you personally guarantee the corporation's obligation.

In other words, if the corporation goes out of business before it has met its obligation under a particular contract, (for example, if the corporation vacates leased space before the end of the lease term) then you may be held personally liable for the remaining obligation.

24

As a defense against any action against you personally for your corporation's obligation, you will need to show that *only* the corporation signed the contract, and that you signed *as president (or other officer) of the corporation* and not individually. (See Chapter 11.)

If you have signed a personal guarantee for any corporate obligation, determine whether it was for a secured debt. In other words, is the creditor able to take the collateral as payment for the balance owed? (Your guarantee may be *conditional*, requiring the creditor to first take the collateral, or *unconditional*, allowing the creditor to come directly to you for payment regardless of the collateral.)

While your guarantee of payment might not require the creditor to first take the collateral in satisfaction of the debt, the creditor may be willing to do so to minimize any potential losses, particularly if the creditor believes that you personally may not be able to pay the amount due.

Personal Guarantee

As for business leases that you have personally guaranteed, the landlord may be obligated to minimize its losses by finding another tenant as quickly as possible. (State laws vary on this issue.) However, any landlord attempting to obtain a judgment against you personally for the balance due on a lease may find the court much more receptive if he or she can show that he or she made a diligent effort to re-lease the space. You should do your best to help the landlord in finding a new tenant to minimize your liability under the guarantee. Even if the law does not require the landlord to attempt to minimize damages, your efforts may discourage the landlord from proceeding against you for the full amount due on the lease.

If there is any question as to whether the guarantee is legally valid and enforceable by the landlord, you should discuss this with an attorney.

Joint Liability

If you have signed a document for payment of an obligation containing the words "joint and several liability," along with other owners of your business, do not assume that you will be responsible for repayment only to the extent of your share in the business. *Joint and several liability* means that each of those individuals who signed the document are individually as well as jointly liable for the total amount due. You may be liable for the entire amount due if the other *guarantors* do not pay.

Creditors usually pursue the signor with the greatest ability to repay the debt. If the creditor pursues you, make him aware of your personal financial situation. You may be able to reach an agreement with the creditor for payment, then pursue the other guarantors for *indemnification,* or reimbursement.

Payroll Taxes

Aside from the corporate obligations you may have personally guaranteed, you must keep in mind that as an officer of the corporation, owner of the business, or partner in a partnership, you have other responsibilities and liabilities. The most important of these are payroll taxes.

As the business owner or authorized signer on the account from which payroll taxes are paid, you are personally obligated for the amount that the business deducted from the employees' wages and failed to send to the Internal Revenue Service (IRS.) In other words, if your bookkeeper fails to make the deposits when due, or if the business ceases operation and taxes are still owed, you may be held personally liable for payment. If this is in fact the case, you should consider the same suggestions for dealing with the IRS. (See Chapter 6.)

STUDENT LOANS

Federal Loan

If you had financial help with your college expenses through a student loan, chances are that repayment was guaranteed by the federal government. In other words, if the loan was made to you by a bank and you failed to pay, the bank looked to the federal government for the money.

Sallie Mae. Following either your graduation or withdrawal from school, you had a grace period (typically six months) before beginning to repay the loan. The bank, school or other lender could collect the loan itself, or could sell the loan to the Student Loan Marketing Association (SLMA, or "Sallie Mae") for collection. The SLMA is a corporation set up by the federal government for the purpose of collecting outstanding student loan obligations. The U.S. Department of Education may attempt to collect the balance due if SLMA is unsuccessful.

Both SLMA and the U.S. Department of Education will report your delinquent student loans to the credit reporting agencies (credit bureaus), and may take other action such as to sue for collection or intercept your income tax refunds.

Default. If you are in default on a federally guaranteed loan, but are now able to start making payments, you may be able to bring the loan out of default by making a certain number of regular, consecutive monthly payments. Contact the guarantee agency that has your loan to find out how to bring the loan out of default.

Private Loan

If you borrowed money from your college or university and the loan was not federally guaranteed, the same options are open to the institution as to any other creditor, such as reporting your delinquent account to a credit reporting agency, hiring a collection agency, and filing a lawsuit. The school may also refuse to give your transcript and your diploma to you, as well as refuse to allow you to re-enroll. On the other hand, you have the same options as with any other creditor, including negotiating a smaller payment amount.

Your Options

Your options will depend upon the type of student loan. The types of federally-guaranteed student loans include the following:

Perkins Loan - based upon need, the loan is made by the school and with federal funds;

Stafford Loan - unsubsidized (interest is charged from the date the loan is disbursed); and

Stafford Loan - subsidized (given on the basis of financial need - the interest is paid by the federal government until repayment begins).

In addition, *Parent PLUS* loans assist parents in paying the expenses of an undergraduate student. U.S. Public Health Service loans are also available to students in health-related studies.

Each of these programs has its own unique rules regarding repayment and collection.

Depending upon the type of loan you have, you may have one or more of the following options if you are unable to pay:

- cancellation of the loan;
- deferment of payments;
- negotiating for temporary suspension or reduction of payments;
- consolidating your loans; or
- filing for bankruptcy (only in case of extreme hardship.)

We will now consider each of these separately.

Cancellation. Again depending upon the type of loan, full or partial cancellation is generally available if you:

- die or become disabled;
- serve in the U.S. military;
- are employed full-time as a nurse, medical technician, or law enforcement or corrections officer;
- are a Peace Corps or VISTA volunteer;

- are a Head Start program staff member;

- are a teacher in certain low-income areas, of handicapped children, or of math, science, foreign languages or in other designated "teacher-shortage" areas; or

- return to school to study at least half time.

For more information, call the holder of your loan or the U.S. Department of Education at 800-621-3115.

Cancellation of the debt may also be possible in certain cases of fraud or misrepresentation by a trade school. In the past, there were numerous trade schools (for such occupations as truck driving, cosmetology, computer operation and repair, etc.) that got students to take out a government loan and turn the money over to the school, then closed the school before the course was completed. Other schools failed to provide sufficient education to allow the student to obtain employment once the course was completed.

If your trade school closed before you could complete the course of study, you were falsely certified to be eligible for the program, or you were entitled to a refund you never got, you may be able to have your loan cancelled. For more information contact the Department of Education and ask for a list of closed schools, or contact your state's Attorney General's office.

Deferment. Typical situations in which *deferment* may be allowed are where you are:

- enrolled in school;

- unemployed;

- on active duty with the military or NOAA;

- a full-time teacher in a teacher-shortage area;
- disabled;
- completing an internship program;
- on parental leave;
- the mother of preschool children; or
- suffering economic hardship.

Depending upon the type of loan, the deferment may be of both principle and interest, or of just principle (meaning you will have to make interest-only payment for the deferment period). For more information, contact your loan holder. Ask for a deferment application.

Negotiation. As with any other loan, you can always contact the holder of the loan, explain your situation, and try to arrange for payments to be temporarily suspended or reduced. If you do not have any luck negotiating an arrangement you can live with, contact your local Consumer Credit Counseling Service. Maybe they will be able to negotiate a better deal.

Consolidation. If you have more than one student loan, you may be able to *consolidate* them at a lower interest rate with a lower single payment, and possibly qualify for a deferment. Much will depend upon the types of loans you have, and whether you are in default. For more information contact the holder of your loan, or Sallie Mae at 800-524-9100. The website for Sallie Mae is **http://www.salliemae.com**. You may also contact the U.S. Department of Education, Federal Direct Loan Program, at 800-494-0979, or

http://www.ed.gov/offices/OSFAP/students/student.html

Bankruptcy. You will generally hear it said that student loans cannot be discharged in bankruptcy. A student loan may be discharged in bankruptcy only if repayment would cause extreme hardship. However, there are a couple of exceptions to this rule, and even if you can not get a discharge you may be able to get some indirect help.

It may be possible to have a student loan discharged in bankruptcy if the payments first became due more than seven years before filing for bankruptcy, or if you can convince the judge that repayment of the loan would cause you undue hardship. If you file for a repayment plan under Chapter 13 of the Bankruptcy Code, and include your student loan in your repayment plan, it will at least stop lawsuits and other harassment over the delinquent loan. Also, if your school is withholding your transcript because of your non-payment, it will have to release the transcript once you notify it of the bankruptcy proceeding, regardless of whether the debt is discharged.

CHILD SUPPORT

A child support obligation is not to be taken lightly. Congress has taken a special interest in payment of child support, and addressed the problem of non-payment by passing the Federal Family Support Act of 1988 and the Revised Uniform Reciprocal Enforcement of Support Act (URESA). In 1997, as part of the Welfare Reform Act, Congress passed the Uniform Interstate Family Support Act (UIFSA), which is more streamlined and gives the states less latitude in enforcement as did the URESA. Under UIFSA, the District Attorney in your state will be contacted by the District Attorney in your spouse's state regarding the child support due. The District Attorney in your state will then pursue you for the amount.

The law requires your employer to honor a court order to withhold the support payment from your wages. (You can also agree with the other parent or guardian of the child to pay directly.) Remember that you can also be ordered to go to jail for contempt of court if you fail to pay child support, and in some states you may be charged with a misdemeanor.

Modification

If you simply cannot pay the amount ordered by the court, then you should file a request for modification, explaining the circumstances and why you believe the amount should be reduced. In all states you will generally need to show that your income has decreased so that you are no longer able to pay the amount originally ordered. A sample Motion for Modification is found at the end of Chapter 12, with examples of reasons for the request. This sample form shows you how simple it can be to ask for a decrease in child support. You should also obtain a copy of your state's support guidelines.

Depending upon your state, the guidelines will be in either the statutes, court rules, or a document from some state agency. If you cannot find them in the statutes or court rules, request a copy from the court clerk or child support enforcement agency. You may find that you are paying more than the guidelines require. If so, you can request a modification.

Judgment

If your spouse gets a judgment against you for past-due child support, that judgment may also be collected like any other judgment and the same time periods for collection may apply. (See Chapter 13.)

Income Tax Refund

In addition, your income tax refunds may be intercepted and applied to your past due child support. If this occurs, you will receive a notice of the impending tax intercept. The notice will advise you of your right to request some kind of hearing to challenge the taking of your tax refund, and how to go about getting a hearing.

Generally, you will only be able to stop the intercept if you have already paid what is owed, or are making regular payments pursuant to an agreement you made for payment of the past due amount (of course, other unusual circumstances may also avoid an intercept, but these are so varied and unusual that they cannot be covered here).

If you are remarried and some of the tax refund is for the income of your current spouse, you can apply to the IRS for your spouse's share of the refund. Contact the IRS to obtain the proper form at:

http://www.irs.ustreas.gov

or

800-899-3676.

STRATEGIES BEFORE CREDITORS AND COLLECTORS CALL 3

PREPARE YOURSELF AND YOUR CREDITORS

As soon as you realize that you may have difficulties in making your payments, you should contact your creditors. Do not try to hide your financial condition. Let them know what has happened—job lay-off, divorce, illness, etc.—and that you will make every effort to meet your financial obligations. Offer to make minimal payments for a period of time, or perhaps *suspend* your payments (not make any) for a month or more.

Generally, your creditors will be much more receptive to your suggestions for reduced or suspended payments if you notify them before they find it necessary to contact you. (Many will accept token payments instead of pursuing collection as long as you explain the reasons for your inability to pay, and that you will make up the difference as soon as you are able.)

Prioritize
You should also take stock of your current financial situation and place your debts and assets in order of priority. (See

Chapter 17.) Your most important obligations may be your mortgage or rent, utilities, and car payment. Consider what you can sell in order to pay off some of your debt. Practical strategies, although perhaps a bit difficult to accept at first, will help see you through the tough times. Perhaps you should sell your car, pay off the loan and buy an older, used car, which would also lower your insurance premium. However, before selling any property to pay your debt, be sure you understand what will be exempt from judgment creditors and bankruptcy in your state. (See Chapter 16.)

THE "MINIMUM ONE DOLLAR PAYMENT" MYTH

Some people have the mistaken notion that a payment of one dollar per month is sufficient—particularly when it comes to hospital and doctor bills—and that no action can be taken by the creditor if that one dollar payment is made regularly. This is an incorrect assumption. Those creditors have the right to receive payment from you in the manner you agreed to pay them, or in a timely manner.

If you cannot reach an agreement with your creditor as to how a past-due account can be paid, or if you reach an agreement and then do not pay, the creditor can send the past-due account to a collection agency, and ultimately (or in some cases directly) to the credit bureau. The creditor may also choose to pursue a judgment against you, often in a small claims court where cases can be handled without a lawyer. However, if your creditor refuses to work with you during your period of financial difficulties, then you may have a more sympathetic judge when you appear in court.

WAGE ASSIGNMENTS

Be wary if a creditor asks you to assign some of your wages to make the payments on the loan. This may be illegal in certain cases under federal law, and it effectively reduces your control over your income. *Wage assignments* in non-real estate transactions are allowed only if you are also given the power to revoke the assignment. (Code of Federal Regulations, Title 16, Section 444.2.)

CREDIT COUNSELING

Consumer Credit Counseling
Consumer credit counseling is available through local offices affiliated with the National Foundation for Consumer Credit. This is a national network of over 1,450 Neighborhood Financial Care Centers. It is a non-profit organization, supported by contributions from banks, consumer finance companies, merchants, credit unions, etc. A Consumer Credit Counseling Service can work with your creditors to establish a realistic payment program. You may find information about the services or locate your nearest center on the Internet at:

http://www.nfcc.org

HUD Counseling
There are approximately 750 HUD (Housing and Urban Development) approved counseling agencies all over the

country. If you are unable to make payments under an FHA (Federal Housing Administration) mortgage, you will be referred to such an agency. However, counseling assistance is available to anyone, usually at no charge. The counselors can help you get employment, budget your income, and work out your credit difficulties. You may call 800-569-4287 for a referral to your local HUD-approved counseling agency, or call 888-HOME-4-US for additional information. You'll also find information at:

http://www.hudhcc.org

WHEN THE COLLECTION AGENCY CALLS 4

A *collection agency* is a business that collects outstanding bills for other businesses.

NOTE: *Child support payments are not "debts" covered by the Fair Debt Collection Practices Act, which is discussed in this chapter.*

After sending past-due notices and perhaps telephoning, a creditor is unable to collect an outstanding bill from you. The creditor will either contract with a collection agency to collect the bill for the creditor, giving the agency a commission from the amount collected (usually fifty percent), with the remaining amount then paid to your creditor. Or, the creditor may sell your account to the collection agency at a discount. When the account has been sold to the agency, the agency can sue on its own behalf to collect the amount due.

WHAT A COLLECTION AGENCY CAN DO

Beyond sending letters and calling, there is little a collection agency can do to collect a debt. An agency collector once said, if people knew their legal rights, collection agencies might find it difficult to stay in business. You should be aware that if a collection agency is a member of a credit reporting service, then your unpaid debt may be reported and may be reflected on your credit report for a period of seven years. (This will be explained in more detail in the next chapter.) Since the collection agency gets paid only on the amounts collected, the collector may use various (and possibly illegal) tactics to get payment from you. Collection agency practices are regulated by the Fair Debt Collection Practices Act (FDCPA).

The Fair Debt Collection Practices Act is a federal law also known as Public Law 95-109. Congress passed this law to regulate collection agencies and help eliminate abusive debt collection practices that contributed to loss of jobs and invasion of privacy.

If a collection agency violates any of the provisions of the law in attempting to collect a debt from you, you may have civil remedies available to you, including *punitive damages*. (In order for the Act to apply, the debt must have been incurred for personal, family, or household purposes.) The Federal Trade Commission is the federal agency responsible for regulating collection agencies. Under the FDCPA, an attorney or law firm can be considered a collection agency if it regularly engages in the collection of debts allegedly owed by consumers.

THE FIRST CALL FROM A COLLECTOR

Before or no later than five days after your first call from the collection agency, the collector must send you a written notice containing:

- the amount of the debt you supposedly owe;
- the name of the creditor to whom the debt is owed;
- a statement that, unless you dispute the validity of the debt within thirty days, the debt will be assumed to be valid;
- a statement that, if you notify the collector in writing within the thirty-day period that the debt, or any portion of it, is disputed, the collector will get verification and mail it to you; and
- a statement that, upon your written request within the thirty-day period, the collector will provide you with the name of the original creditor if different from the current creditor.

Any communication you receive from the collector must clearly state that the purpose of the communication is to collect a debt, and that any information obtained will be used for that purpose.

You have thirty days after receipt of the notice from the collection agency to respond. Send a letter back to the agency stating that you do not agree with all or part of the bill, and why, in your opinion, you do not owe the money. (See page 55 for a sample letter.)

NOTE: *Any subsequent communication by the collector regarding the debt must also include the fact that you have disputed the debt.*

The collection agency must then stop all attempts to collect the debt from you until the debt is verified by the   and a copy of the verification is sent to you. You may demand that the collector notify any person who received notice of the debt from him within the previous ninety-day period, that the debt has been disputed.

If you do not dispute the debt in writing within the thirty-day period, the collection agency can assume you agree that the amount stated in the notice is accurate, and can continue its collection efforts.

When you receive a call or letter from a collection agency attempting to collect a debt you owed to someone else, there are a number of things you can do. Most importantly, you can simply write a letter and ask that you not be contacted anymore.(See page 54 for a sample of this type of letter.) This, by law, should be enough. However, some collectors use very aggressive and sometimes abusive tactics in order to get payments.

WHAT A COLLECTION AGENCY <u>CANNOT</u> DO

The following is a list of collection agency practices that are among those prohibited under the Fair Debt Collection Practices Act (FDCPA), with suggestions as to what you can do if you believe an agency has violated a provision of the Act.

Remember that these apply to collection agencies, and not the creditor to whom the debt may be owed. While the creditor cannot harass you, he is not subject to the same regulations as collection agencies. (Several states regulate the activities of creditors as well.)

NOTE: *These are items that the FDCPA states the collection agencies <u>cannot</u> do. The statements are summarized.*

FDCPA Statement: A collection agency representative *should not* lead you to believe in any manner that he is a law enforcement officer or a representative of any governmental agency. A debt collector is prohibited from using a police badge or other symbol of authority.

Response: If you are contacted by a debt collector using these tactics, make sure you get his name and place of employment to use in any action against him.

FDCPA Statement: A collection agency representative *must not* use or threaten force, violence, or other criminal means to harm you, your reputation, or property.

Response: If a debt collector threatens to cause you harm, then you should, if possible, record the conversation and advise the collector that you are doing so, or ask a friend to listen to the call on an extension phone. Some collection agencies record telephone conversations their collectors have with debtors in order to minimize these violations.

FDCPA Statement: A collection agency representative *must not* communicate with other people (except your lawyer or a consumer reporting agency) about your account without your prior consent except to the extent reasonably necessary to enforce a court order.

Response: If a collector violates this law, have the individual to whom the information was disclosed write down that information, sign it and have it notarized. You may then use this to support your complaint to the appropriate governmental office. You may also have a claim for damages.

FDCPA Statement: A collection agency representative *must not* communicate with you at any unusual time or place or at a time or place that the collector should know would be inconvenient to you. Unless the collector has knowledge of circumstances to the contrary, he should assume that the most convenient time for contacting you is between the hours of 8:00 a.m. and 9:00 p.m.

> **Response:** If the collector calls you before 8:00 a.m. and after 9:00 p.m. (unless he knows you have odd working hours, such as an evening shift, or that other unusual circumstances exist), he is violating the Fair Debt Collection Practices Act. First advise the collector in writing that this is a violation; if it continues, then it can be reported to the Federal Trade Commission.

FDCPA Statement: A debt collector *should not* contact you at your place of employment if he knows or has reason to know that your employer prohibits such calls.

> **Response:** If a collector contacts you at your place of employment, you can stop the calls by sending a letter to the collection agency advising the agency employees not to contact you at work. You should send this letter certified mail, return receipt requested, so the collection agency cannot dispute having received your letter.
>
> If you tell the collector, in writing, that you refuse to pay the debt or that you want the collector to stop calling or contacting you, the collector should not communicate with you further except to:
> - advise you that he is stopping his efforts to collect the debt;

- notify you that the collector or creditor may pursue other remedies ordinarily available, such as filing a lawsuit or notifying a credit reporting agency; or

- notify you that the collector or creditor will be taking a specific action regarding the debt, such as reporting it to the credit bureau.

FDCPA Statement: A collection agency representative *must not* communicate or threaten to communicate to anyone credit information about you that he knows or should know is false. If you are disputing the debt, any communication regarding the debt by the collector must also include the fact that you are disputing it.

    Response: If the collector talks to or otherwise communicates with anyone about your credit, he cannot by law give any information that he knows or should know is incorrect. If you are aware of such communication, be sure to document it in writing and notify the collector and the FTC.

FDCPA Statement: A collection agency representative *must not* willfully communicate with you or any member of your family so frequently as could reasonably be expected to harass you or your family, or willfully engage in other conduct that can reasonably be expected to annoy, abuse, or harass you or any member of your family.

    Response: If you get continuous telephone calls, you should keep track and write down the date and time of day for each call. To stop the continuous calls, write and send a letter to the agency, certified mail, return receipt requested, notifying the agency to stop contacting you. Once your letter is received by the agency, an agency collector is prohibited from contacting you again except to notify you that (a) contact will stop, or (b) that the agency is pursuing a specific remedy. A specific remedy might be that your debt will be assigned to a credit reporting agency.

FDCPA Statement: A collection agency representative *shall not* use profane, obscene, vulgar, or willfully abusive language in communicating with you or any member of your family.

Response: If a debt collector uses profanity when calling you about payment of your debt, record the conversation, if possible, and let the collector know that the conversation is being recorded. Without the recording or some evidence of the language used, it is difficult to support your claim against the collector. You should also notify the creditor (the person to whom the debt was first owed) that the agency collector is using profanity in communications with you. The creditor might just recall your account (and other accounts) from the collection agency.

FDCPA Statement: A collection agency representative *must not*, in order to embarrass or disgrace you, falsely represent or imply that you have committed a crime or other misconduct.

Response: If the collector tells you that you have committed a crime, or that you are otherwise guilty of misconduct, ask him or her to explain the particular statute or law you have violated. Tell the collector that he or she should provide that information in writing. Keep track of your communication with the collector.

FDCPA Statement: A collection agency representative *must not* use any written communication that appears to be a legal document or that gives the appearance of being authorized, issued, or approved by a government, or governmental agency including the police when it is not. This includes any document that looks like a court order, judgment, or a subpoena. They must not misrepresent that documents are illegal or do not require a response from you when in fact they do.

> **Response:** If a collection agency representative contacts you with any such type of documentation, be sure to keep a copy, then send it, along with your letter of explanation, to the FTC.

On the other hand, make sure that if you do in fact receive a legal document you respond appropriately.

FDCPA Statement: A collection agency representative *shall not* communicate with you under the guise of an attorney by using the stationery of an attorney or forms or instruments that only attorneys are authorized to prepare.

> **Response:** A collection agency is prohibited from using a collection letter that falsely appears as though it was prepared by an attorney. A debt collector cannot send a collection letter from a legal department when no such department exists. If you have any doubt, ask to speak to the agency's attorney, and follow up with an inquiry to your local bar association. You should be able to ascertain whether or not the collection agency is trying to mislead you.

FDCPA Statement: A collection agency representative *shall not* orally communicate with you in such a manner as to give the false impression or appearance that he is—or is associated with—an attorney.

> **Response:** If a debt collector calls and even implies that he is affiliated with an attorney, ask the collector to send you a letter on the attorney's stationery. If the collector has falsely stated or implied that he is associated with an attorney, he has violated this provision. (If possible, also record the conversation for future use—after you have told the collector that the conversation is being recorded.)

FDCPA Statement: A collection agency representative *must not* advertise or threaten to advertise your account for sale in an effort to force you to pay, or falsely tell you that the account has been sold to a third party.

> **Response:** Demand that the collector provide you with written information regarding the advertisement, and/or the name and address of the party to when the account has been sold. Keep this documentation to file a complaint or lawsuit against the agency.

FDCPA Statement: A collection agency representative *must not* publish or post or threaten you that he will publish or post, individual names or any list of names of consumers, commonly known as a "deadbeat list," for the purpose of enforcing or attempting to enforce collection of your debt.

> **Response:** Publishing your name as a debtor to force you into paying a debt is prohibited. If a collector threatens to place your name on a deadbeat list or in any manner make your debt public information, ask the collector to notify you in writing. If you receive such a letter, or have knowledge that

the collector has in fact published your name, you may have a claim for damages.

FDCPA Statement: A collection agency representative *must not* refuse to provide adequate identification of himself or his employer or other entity whom he represents when you ask him to do so.

Response: A debt collector must give you his correct name and the correct name of his company when asked. Ask the collector to send you a statement on his company's letterhead containing his signature.

FDCPA Statement: A collection agency representative *must not* mail any communication to you in an envelope or post card with words typed, written, or printed on the outside of the envelope or post card calculated to embarrass you.

Response: A debt collector is prohibited from mailing you an envelope or postcard that is intended to embarrass you into paying the debt. This includes language such as to "Deadbeat John Doe." If you receive correspondence that implies that you owe an outstanding debt, then you may have a claim for damages.

Example: A woman in Utah was able to sue a collection agency for making harassing phone calls and sending a "Wanted" poster to her employer and family saying she was a "deadbeat parent" because she was behind on her child support payments.

Collectors are also prohibited from making false misrepresentations or implying that they either are, or work for, a consumer reporting agency (although some collection agencies are in fact affiliated or associated with reporting agencies).

Miscellaneous Unfair Practices

It is considered an unfair practice for a collector to collect or attempt to collect any amount not specifically spelled out in the agreement creating the debt.

Example: Interest cannot be charged unless you initially agreed to pay it when you incurred the debt.

Accepting checks postdated more than five days is prohibited unless the collection agency notifies you no more than ten and no less than three days before that the check will be deposited.

A collection agency cannot cause you to be charged with any expenses, such as collect telephone calls, without first disclosing to you the reason for the call.

A collection agency cannot falsely threaten to take your property if it has no authority or intent to do so or if the property is exempt (see Chapter 16).

IF YOU HAVE AN ATTORNEY

If you have employed an attorney, you must provide the collection agency with the attorney's name and address. The agency must then send all correspondence directly to the attorney, and not to you.

WHAT YOU CAN DO ON YOUR OWN

The more knowledgeable you are about what a collection agency can and cannot do, the better equipped you will be to fight back. When contacted by a collection agency representative, keep track of the methods used to contact you, including the dates, times, and places. If at all possible, have a witness. If you believe that a collection agency has violated any of the above laws, you have several options.

You should make it clear to the collection agency representative that you are aware of the laws, and believe they have been violated.

You may file a lawsuit for the amount of actual damages you have suffered, and additional damages up to $1,000.00. In assessing your damages, the court will consider:

- the frequency and persistence of the violations by the debt collector;
- the nature of the violations;
- and the extent to which they were intentional. If you are successful, you will also be entitled to your court costs and attorneys fees. The collector may not be held liable if he can prove to the court that the violation was not intentional and resulted from an honest mistake.

Example: In a Texas case in 1995, a jury awarded a couple $11 million in a lawsuit against a credit card company for the abusive practices of its collection agency in attempting to collect a $2,000 debt. Collectors had made repetitious phone calls and used profanity, called the debtor's office thirty-six times in one hour, threatened to disrupt the debtor's work with bomb threats, and threatened to have them killed.

In any legal action by a collection agency to collect a debt, you can use a violation of the Fair Debt Collection Practices Act as a defense.

You may file a complaint with your state Attorney General's office, or the particular government office in your state that handles collection agencies—often a consumer affairs office. (See Appendix B.) You may also register a complaint with the office of the Federal Trade Commission (FTC) nearest you. (See the sample letter on page 56.)

Finally, if you truly owe the debt and the debt collector is making legitimate, legal contact, remember that most agencies will be willing to work with you in your efforts to clear up past-due accounts. If you tell the collector that you simply are unable to pay the entire balance due, you should be able to reach an agreeable payment plan or pay a lump-sum reduced amount. Remember, it is in the agency's interest to get money in as quickly as possible. A reduced lump-sum total payment may be much more attractive than small payments extended over a long period of time.

FOR FURTHER RESEARCH

The Fair Debt Collection Practices Act is found in United States Code, Title 15, Sections 1692:

> 1692(a)
>
> 1692(b) "Acquisition of location information"
>
> 1692(c) "Communication in connection with debt collection"

1692(d) "Harassment or abuse"

1692(e) "False or misleading representations"

1692(f) "Unfair practices"

1692(g) "Validation of debts"

1692(j) "Furnishing certain deceptive forms."

Other sections of the Act include the legal actions that can be taken by debt collectors, civil liability of the collectors, and enforcement. Information can be obtained directly from the Federal Trade Commission at:

http://www.ftc.gov/bcp/menu-credit.htm

You should also contact your state consumer affairs office for additional information. (See Appendix B.)

SAMPLE LETTER REQUESTING NO CONTACT

July 21, 2001

EZ Collections   CERTIFIED MAIL
123 Short Street   RETURN RECEIPT REQUESTED
Anytown, USA   P-284-398-992

     RE: Account No. 298955-3018

Dear Sir or Madam:

Please do not contact me anymore regarding
the above-referenced debt.

                         Sincerely,

                         Jane Doe

SAMPLE LETTER FOR DISPUTING A BILL

July 21, 2001

EZ Collections   CERTIFIED MAIL
123 Short Street   RETURN RECEIPT REQUESTED
Anytown, USA   P-284-398-993

   RE: Account No. 298955-3018

Dear Sir or Madam:

I am disputing the validity of the above-
referenced debt for the following reason:

My account with Dr. Painless was paid in
full on August 31, 2000.

                    Sincerely,

                    Jane Doe

Two other examples of reasons for disputing:

"I have never had work done by ABC Drain
Cleaners."

"The service provided by Mr. Smith was
inadequate and not as represented by him."

SAMPLE LETTER TO FTC

August 2, 2001

Federal Trade Commission
1718 Peachtree St., N.W., Room 1000
Atlanta, GA 30367

    RE: EZ Collections
        123 Short Street
        Anytown, USA

Dear Sir or Madam:

On January 15, 2001, I received a letter from EZ Collections claiming I owed $50.00 to a Dr. Payne. I received a telephone call from an EZ Collections employee on April 30, 2001, demanding payment of the $50.00.

I then wrote to EZ Collections, stating that I do not know a Dr. Payne, that I was never a patient of his, and that I do not owe the $50.00.

The EZ Collections employee continued to call me and demand payment, often late at night (after 9:00 p.m.).

I am hereby making a complaint against EZ Collections for violating the Fair Debt Collection Practices Act.

                 Sincerely,

                 Jane Doe
cc: EZ Collections

CONSUMER REPORTING AGENCIES AND YOUR CREDIT REPORT 5

The Fair Credit Reporting Act as amended September 30, 1997 (U.S.C., Title 15, Sec. 1601.) regulates the activities of credit reporting agencies. A credit reporting agency, also known as a credit bureau and called *consumer reporting agency* under this law, means any person or business that assembles or evaluates consumer credit information for the purpose of providing consumer reports (commonly known as *credit reports*) to third parties. Under the Fair Credit Reporting Act (FCRA), *consumer* means an individual. You, as the person whose credit is being reported, are the consumer.

INFORMATION A CONSUMER REPORTING AGENCY MAY FURNISH

A reporting agency may furnish your credit report only under circumstances provided for by law, which are the following:

- in response to a court order;
- in accordance with written instructions from the consumer;

- to any person that the reporting agency has reason to believe:
  - is involved in the extension of credit to, or review or collection of an account of the consumer; or
  - intends to use the information for employment purposes; or
  - intends to use the information in connection with the underwriting of insurance involving the consumer; or
  - intends to use the information in connection with a determination of the consumer's eligibility for a license or other benefit granted by a governmental agency (if the agency is required by law to consider an applicant's financial responsibility or status); or
  - otherwise has a legitimate business need for the information in connection with a business transaction involving the consumer; or
  - in certain cases involving child support issues.

OBTAINING INFORMATION FROM THE AGENCY'S FILES

The contents of your credit report can affect your ability to get a loan as well as employment. As a consumer, upon request and proper identification, you have the right to obtain the following information in the reporting agency's files:

- the nature and substance of all information (except medical information) in the agency's file on the consumer at the time of the request;

- the sources of the information (except as to information acquired solely for use in preparing an investigative consumer report and used for no other purpose, which is beyond the scope of this book);
- the recipients of any consumer report on the consumer that the reporting agency has furnished:
  - for employment purposes within the two-year period preceding the request; and
  - for any other purpose within the six-month period preceding the request.

The agency is required to provide you the requested information during normal business hours and on reasonable notice. The information should be provided to you in person if you have proper identification, or by telephone if you have made written request and have proper identification. If long distance, you must pay for the call. The agency must have trained personnel explain to you any questions you have about the report. If you make the request in person and have someone with you, the agency must have written permission from you to *disclose* any information in your companion's presence. The three major national credit bureaus are:

Equifax
P.O. Box 740241
Atlanta, GA 30374-0241
800-685-1111

Experian (formerly TRW)
P.O. Box 2002
Allen, TX 75013
888-397-3742

TransUnion
P.O. Box 1000
Chester, PA 19022
800-916-8800

ITEMS YOUR REPORT CANNOT CONTAIN

By law, your report cannot contain any of the following:

- a discharge or final order in Bankruptcy Court dated more than ten years prior to the date of the credit report;

- lawsuits and judgments entered more than seven years prior to the date of the credit report. (However, if the applicable statute of limitations is longer than seven years, lawsuits and judgments may stay on the credit report until the applicable statute of limitations expire. For example, if your state allows a judgment to remain in effect for a period of ten years, then the ten-year period may apply, instead of the seven-year period.);

- paid tax liens which, from the date of payment, precede the report by more than seven years;

- accounts placed for collection or charged to profit and loss by the creditor that are dated more than seven years before the credit report;

- records of arrest, indictment, or conviction of crime that, from date of disposition, release, or parole, precede the report by more than seven years; and

- any other adverse information that precedes the report by more than seven years;

- default information concerning U.S. Government insured or guaranteed student loans can be reported for seven years after actions to collect the debt have been taken against certain guarantors.

However, the above restrictions do not apply if the report is to be used in connection with:

- a credit transaction involving, or which may reasonably be expected to involve, a principal amount of $150,000.00 or more;

- the underwriting of life insurance involving, or that may reasonably be expected to involve, a face amount of $150,000.00 or more; or

- the employment of any individual at an annual salary that equals, or that may reasonably be expected to equal, $75,000.00 or more.

THE "QUICK-FIX"

You may be told by a so-called "credit repair" company that you will not be able to get credit for ten years after you have filed for bankruptcy. Such companies are regulated under the Credit Repair Organizations Act. (U.S.C., Title 15, Chapter 41.) If you have been granted bankruptcy, you might receive correspondence from credit repair companies explaining that you will be unable to get loans, credit cards, etc. This, of course, is not necessarily correct. It may be suggested that the credit repair company can help you hide your bankruptcy by essentially providing you with a new credit history.

Warning: To help you "hide" your bankruptcy, the credit repair company may promise to tell you how, for a fee, to establish a new credit identity. The plan, however, is illegal. If you use the plan, often called *file segregation*, you could face fines or even prison.

If the company offers to assist you in hiding your bankruptcy and establish a new credit identity beware that this is probably illegal, particularly if you are to apply for a new tax identification number to use in place of your social security number, using a new address and credit references.

Remember that no one can legally remove correct negative information from your credit report. However, the law does allow you the opportunity to ask that incorrect or incomplete information be reviewed as explained in this chapter. You can also submit a letter of explanation, which is to be included with a copy of your credit report. There is no charge for this. Anything that a so-called credit repair service can do for you legally, you can do for yourself at little or no cost.

Disputing Items in Your Report

The information contained in credit reports is obtained from a variety of sources, including local court records and businesses who pay a fee to the credit bureau. If you dispute the accuracy of any of the information in your credit report, do the following:

- If you dispute the completeness or accuracy of any item of information contained in your file, and you let the reporting agency know of your dispute, the agency must, within a reasonable period of time, reinvestigate and record the current status of that information. If it has reasonable grounds to believe that your dispute is frivolous or irrelevant, then they may be exempted.

- If after the reinvestigation the information is found to be inaccurate or can no longer be verified by the agency, then the agency must promptly delete the information from your report. Contradictory information in the file cannot be used by the agency as reasonable grounds for believing your dispute is frivolous or irrelevant. (See sample letter on page 72.) According to the law, if you disagree with an entry on your credit report and the creditor placing the information on the report cannot verify that it is correct, then the credit reporting service *must* remove that information.

- If the reinvestigation does not resolve the dispute, you may file a brief statement setting forth the nature of the dispute. The agency may limit the statement to not more than one hundred words if agency personnel provide you with assistance in writing a clear summary of the dispute.

- Whenever you file a statement of dispute, unless there are reasonable grounds for the agency to believe your statement is frivolous or irrelevant, the agency must clearly note in any subsequent report containing the information that it is disputed. It must provide either your statement or a clear and accurate summary of your statement. (See the sample letter on page 73.)

Example: John and Sandy made a loan application to purchase a new home. The credit report reflected non-payment of a doctor bill approximately a year previously. John and Sandy thought their insurance company had paid the outstanding bill, and immediately made arrangements to pay once they realized this reflected negatively on their credit report. They also sent a letter to the reporting agency clarifying the reason for non-payment and stating that acceptable arrangements had been made with the physician to pay the bill. They were then given the mortgage they had applied for.

• Following the agency's removal of any information that is found to be inaccurate, whose accuracy can no longer be verified, or any notation in the agency's file as to disputed information, the agency must, at your request, (1) either furnish notification that the item has been deleted or (2) send the statement or summary regarding a disputed item to any person who is specifically designated by you and who has within the past two years received your credit report for employment purposes, or within the last six months received your credit report for any other purposes.

The agency must clearly and conspicuously disclose to you your rights to make such a request. The agency's disclosure must be made at or before the time the information is removed or your statement regarding the disputed information is received.

COST OF THE REPORT

You may request a copy of your report, and it must be provided free of charge, from the reporting agency your report came from if:

- you request it within 60 days of notice that your credit has been or may be adversely affected;

- you request it within 60 days of notice that you have been denied employment; or

- if credit or insurance rates are increased due to the report.

Under the law, credit reporting services can charge no more than $8 for a copy of your credit report. However, this amount may be adjusted in the future for inflation by the Federal Trade Commission (FTC). The agency cannot charge for the deletion of any information that is determined to be inaccurate. Some agencies will provide you with one free copy per year. It may be a good idea for you to obtain a copy once a year to be sure of accuracy.

If you receive welfare, are out of work and looking for a job, or have been the victim of credit card fraud (someone has stolen and used your card), you must be provided a copy of your credit report upon request at no charge.

REPORTS FOR EMPLOYMENT PURPOSES

Under the law, a prospective employer *must* have your written permission before getting a copy of your credit report. A reporting agency that furnishes a report for employment purposes that contains items of information that are matters of *public record* and are likely to have an adverse effect upon your ability to obtain employment *must*:

- at the time such information is reported to a prospective employer, notify you of the fact that public record information is being reported by the consumer reporting agency, together with the name and address of the person to whom such information is being reported; and

- maintain strict procedures designed to insure that whenever public record information that is likely to have an adverse effect on your ability to obtain employment is reported, it is complete and up-to-date. Items relating to arrests, indictments, convictions, suits, tax liens, and outstanding judgments are considered up-to-date if the current public record status of the item at the time of the report is reported.

Reports Containing Medical Information

The law restricts a credit reporting agency from furnishing a credit report that contains any medical information for employment, credit, insurance, or direct marketing transaction purposes without first obtaining your consent.

Requirements for Users of Reports

Whenever credit or insurance for personal, family, household purposes, or employment is denied or the charge for such credit or insurance is increased because of information contained in a report from a reporting agency, the user of the report must advise you and must supply the name and address of the consumer reporting agency making the report.

Businesses sometimes create mailing lists of prospective new customers based on information contained in credit reports, and make firm offers of credit or insurance based on this information. (For example, you may receive offers of a specified line of credit from credit card companies through the mail.)

The law requires that a single toll-free number be established by the three major credit reporting services, Equifax, TransUnion Corporation, and Experian (formerly known as TRW) so that consumers may prohibit the use of their credit reports for credit or insurance transactions that are not initiated by the customer. A notice of election form should be provided to you for completion and signature. The election will be effective only for a two-year period if you do not submit the notice of election form. (Each of the three major credit reporting services also has its own toll-free number.)

USE OF OTHER INFORMATION

Sometimes credit for personal, family, or household purposes is denied or the charge for such credit is increased either wholly or in part because of information obtained from a person, other than a consumer reporting agency. This affects your creditworthiness, credit standing, credit capacity, character, general reputation, personal characteristics, or mode of living, and the user of such information must, within a reasonable period of time after receiving your written request, disclose the nature of the information to you. The user must receive your written request within sixty days of your learning of the adverse action. At the time the user of the information tells you about the adverse action, he must also clearly and accurately disclose your rights to make the written request.

OBTAINING INFORMATION UNDER FALSE PRETENSES

Anyone who knowingly and willfully obtains information about a consumer from a reporting agency under false pretenses can be fined not more than $5,000 or imprisoned not more than two years, or both.

PROVIDING INFORMATION TO AN UNAUTHORIZED PERSON

Any officer or employee of a reporting agency who knowingly and willfully provides information concerning an individual from the agency's files to a person *not authorized to receive that information* can be fined up to $5,000 imprisoned up to one year, or both.

REPORTING AGENCY LIABILITY FOR NON-COMPLIANCE

A credit reporting agency may either comply with the law, which is generally the case and make an unintentional error (*negligent non-compliance*) or intentionally violate the law (*willful non-compliance*). Willful non-compliance carries the greatest penalty.

Negligent Non-Compliance

A reporting agency or user of information provided by a reporting agency that *negligently* fails to comply with any requirement under the *Consumer Credit Act* is liable to you in an amount equal to the sum of:

- any actual damages suffered by you as a result of the failure; and

- in the case of any successful action to enforce any liability under the applicable section of the Consumer Credit Act, the costs of the action together with reasonable attorney's fees as determined by the court.

Willful Non-Compliance

A reporting agency or user of information provided by a reporting agency that *willfully* fails to *comply* with the legal requirements is liable to you under the FCRA in an amount equal to the sum of:

- any actual damages suffered by you as a result of the failure;
- such amount of punitive damages as the court may allow; and
- in the case of any successful action to enforce any liability under this section, the costs of the action together with reasonable attorney's fees as determined by the court.

Your Remedies

If you believe a credit reporting agency has failed to comply with any of the requirements under the Consumer Credit Act, particularly the FCRA, you may have recourse.

Example: Consumers were awarded damages for embarrassment and humiliation as a result of a reporting agency negligently furnishing an inaccurate mortgage report.

Example: A consumer was awarded damages for mental anguish where he had to leave his employment numerous times to meet with the agency as a result of its refusal to disclose information to him about his credit report.

Time Limitations

You may bring an action against the agency within two years from the date the liability arises; *except*, where the agency has willfully misrepresented any information required to be disclosed and the information misrepresented is necessary to establish the agency's liability, the action may be brought within two years after discovery of the misrepresentation.

The FTC is the federal agency given the authority to enforce the provisions of the Fair Credit Reporting Act, and you may register a *complaint* at the office in your district. (See Appendix C.) You should send your complaint in writing, with a copy of the letter going to the credit reporting agency. (See the sample letter on page 74.) The complaint should be sent to:

Consumer Response Center, FCRA
Federal Trade Commission
Washington, D.C. 20580

FOR FURTHER RESEARCH

The Federal Trade Commission has detailed information about credit reporting agencies, and the rules that govern them, available at its website,

http://www.ftc.gov/images/sub_seal.gif

It is also possible to file your complaint on-line at this site. The brochure, Fair Credit Reporting, is also available from the FTC. You can find the Act in Title 15, United States Code, Chapter 41, Subchapter III. Refer to Sections 1681(a) through 1681(u). You should also contact your state's consumer affairs office for additional information.

SAMPLE LETTER REQUESTING REMOVAL OF INFORMATION

August 12, 2001

Credit Bureau   CERTIFIED MAIL
321 Broad Street   RETURN RECEIPT REQUESTED
Your Town, USA   P-298-335-482

    RE: Credit Report for Jane Doe
          Social Security No 555-55-5555

Dear Sir or Madam:

On August 3, 2001, I was notified that credit had been denied me because of an entry on my credit report.

The credit report showed that I failed to make payment in the amount of $50.00 to a Dr. Payne. You must have me confused with another Jane Doe, as I do not know a Dr. Payne, nor have I ever used his services.

Please delete this entry from my credit report. Thank you.

                  Sincerely,

                  Jane Doe

SAMPLE LETTER—
INACCURATE CREDIT INFORMATION

August 12, 2001

Credit Bureau   CERTIFIED MAIL
321 Broad Street   RETURN RECEIPT REQUESTED
Your Town, USA   P-298-335-482

    RE: Credit Report for Jane Doe
         Social Security No 555-55-5555

Dear Sir or Madam:

In making application for a mortgage it
was brought to my attention that there is
an entry on my credit report showing that
I owe Dr. Feilgoodt a balance of $300.

The $300 was for medical treatment approx-
imately one year ago. It was my understanding that this amount had been paid by
my insurance company along with other medical bills incurred at that time. I did
not receive a bill for this amount after
giving the medical center business office
information about my insurance policy.

I intend to pay Dr. Feilgoodt's bill in
full as soon as possible. Please include
this letter in my credit report file.

Thank you.

                    Sincerely,

                    James Roe

SAMPLE LETTER—COMPLAINT TO FTC

August 12, 2001

Federal Trade Commission
1718 Peachtree St., N.W., Room 1000
Atlanta, GA 30367

    RE: Credit Bureau
         321 Broad Street
         Your Town, USA

Dear Sir or Madam:

On June 1, 2001, I notified Credit Bureau, in writing, that an entry on my credit report was incorrect, and asked that it be deleted.

The credit report showed that I failed to make payment in the amount of $50.00 to a Dr. Payne. Apparently Credit Bureau has me confused with another Jane Doe, as I do not know a Dr. Payne, nor have I ever used his services.

Credit Bureau refused to follow up on my letter and the entry still shows on my credit report without an explanation or notice that it is disputed.

I wish to file a complaint against Credit Bureau under the Fair Credit Reporting Act.

                       Sincerely,

                       Jane Doe

cc: Credit Bureau

THE INTERNAL REVENUE SERVICE 6

IRS COLLECTIONS

Unlike other creditors, the IRS has almost unlimited access to your property if you owe a tax bill. The IRS has the authority to take your house (a claim that this is your principal residence, referred to as your "homestead" under state and federal laws, does not matter), your bank accounts, your wages, your business, and virtually anything else you own in order to pay outstanding taxes. As a practical matter, most debts can be worked out with an IRS agent, and a payment plan can be arranged.

As a result of Congressional hearings about the collection tactics used by some Internal Revenue Service employees, a law was passed in 1998 (The Internal Revenue Service Restructuring and Reform Act of 1998), which has generally resulted in fewer tax audits and property seizures. The law requires an oversight board to oversee the activities of the IRS. Congress limited the use of many aggressive collection tactics, and allowed taxpayers to sue examiners. Thus, collectors have in general become more accommodating and empathetic to the plight of the taxpayer.

A national taxpayer advocate was provided for, to take into account the facts in a manner most favorable to the taxpayer (as opposed to the IRS). The instances in which taxpayer assistance orders are issued have been expanded to include:

- instances of immediate threat of adverse action;

- a delay of more than 30 days in solving the taxpayer's problem;

- the payment by the taxpayer of significant cost if relief isn't granted; and

- irreparable injury or tremendous long-standing adverse impact if relief is not granted.

The new law, however, does not mean that you do not have to pay taxes owed. The following pages provide general guidelines for dealing with tax payments.

ASSUMING INCORRECT IRS BILLS

If you get a notice from the IRS stating that you miscalculated your taxes due and that you still owe money, do not panic. First, check the figures. It may well be that the IRS clerk checking your return did the miscalculation. In fact, it is possible that the amount the IRS claims you owe is not actually due. During the busiest tax filing season the IRS hires temporary workers, and many of the full-time entry-level employees who first see your return are poorly trained. It has been estimated that nearly half of the official notices from the IRS demanding additional payments are inaccurate.

You may need help in your recalculations. If you find that the IRS has in fact made a mistake, respond to the notice, in writing, and enclose a copy of your calculations as well as a copy of the IRS notice.

ANSWERING AN IRS INQUIRY

It is of utmost importance that you respond to an IRS inquiry no later than the due date that is written on their correspondence. If you ignore the IRS letters telling you that you owe additional taxes, you will be sent:

- several statements;
- a Notice of Deficiency or a similar notice (depending upon the type of error the IRS claims you made), which gives you an opportunity to protest the IRS assessment by filing your protest in the U.S. Tax Court; and
- an *assessment notice*, which advises you that liens are being filed against all of your property.

These liens remain until the amount due is paid. If you do not respond this time, the IRS agent may begin taking your property after a thirty-day waiting period.

PROPERTY THE IRS CAN TAKE

The IRS has the right to take virtually all of your property without any regard to the equity (except as specifically set forth below.) The IRS agent can take your car, house, bank accounts, and wages.

The IRS can take your property, sell it for just enough to pay the taxes owed and the costs of the sale, without any consideration for the amount of equity you have in it.

TAXPAYERS BILL OF RIGHTS

The Internal Revenue Service Restructuring and Reform Act of 1998 provides greater assistance to taxpayers than did the previous law. The grounds for obtaining a Taxpayer Assistance Order, which provides relief from property seizures or collections, have been expanded as explained above. However, the list is not exclusive, and each case should be judged on its own facts. If you find yourself in such a dire situation, you may apply for such an order by filing IRS Form 911 with an IRS Problem Resolution Officer.

A list of taxpayer assistance offices can be found in the IRS publication 1546. The form is available by calling 800-829-1040 and asking for a Problem Resolution Officer to review your case. This and other information about tax payments, including IRS pamphlets, is also readily available at the consumer-friendly Internal Revenue Service website.

WHAT THE IRS CANNOT TAKE

There are certain items the IRS by law cannot touch. (U.S.C., Title 26, Sec. 6334.) These are:

- wearing apparel and school books for you or members of your family;

- fuel, food, furniture and personal effects totalling $6250;
- so many of the books and tools necessary for your trade, business or profession that do not exceed $3125 total in value;
- unemployment benefits;
- mail addressed to any person (but not yet delivered);
- certain annuity and pension payments under the Railroad Retirement Act, benefits under the Railroad Unemployment Insurance Act, special pension payments received by a person whose name has been entered on the Army, Navy, Air Force, and Coast Guard Medal of Honor roll, and annuities based on retired or retainer pay;
- workman's compensation benefits;
- judgments for support of minor children (if you have been ordered to pay, the amount necessary for you to comply with judgment is exempt);
- minimum exemption for wages, salary, and other income calculated as the aggregate amount of the deductions for personal exemptions allowed in the tax year in which the tax levy occurs, divided by 52 (If you do not submit a written and verified statement to the IRS specifying the facts necessary to determine the proper amount, the exemption will be applied as if you were a married individual filing a separate return with only one exemption);
- certain service-connected disability payments;
- certain public assistance payments; and
- assistance under the Job Training Partnership Act.

Your primary residence may be exempt *unless* the district or assistant district IRS director approves the levy on your property or the Secretary of the IRS finds that collection of the tax is in jeopardy.

IRS TIME LIMITATIONS

The IRS can come after you for additional taxes only three years after you filed the return. However, if the IRS finds that the gross income shown on your return was twenty-five percent less than the actual amount, the time limitation is increased to six years. If you failed to file or filed a fraudulent return, there is no time limitation.

AUDITS

Every year a certain number of tax returns are chosen by the IRS for an audit. An *audit* simply means an official examination and verification of your financial accounts and records. A return may be selected for audit because of certain information it contains—such as deductions for home office expenses—or it may be a random selection. Audits are made by correspondence (you are asked to send in supporting evidence of figures), in an IRS examiner's office, or at your home or office.

To prepare for an audit of your tax return you should make sure that all your records are in order and that the figures on your tax return can be supported by documentation. In other words, if you have deducted costs for entertainment as a business expense, you should be able to clearly show the IRS examiner that the entertainment was in fact for a business purpose. Similarly, if you have deducted expenses for maintaining a portion of your home as an office, be able to show that the area is being used exclusively for your business.

Representation

You may want to have someone represent you at the audit—an accountant, your bookkeeper, or in some cases, an attorney—removing you from the immediate scrutiny and questioning of the examiner. You do not have to be physically present at the audit. Your representative can come back to you for clarification of any items questioned by the examiner and give you an opportunity to put some forethought into your response. If you do go alone and questions come up that you are unable to answer adequately, then you can tell the examiner that you will have to consult with your accountant or other tax advisor.

Preparation

Although the majority of audits result in the taxpayer owing money, it is not always the case. The important point to remember is to be prepared. Of course, preparation should begin long before you receive notice of an audit. Keep accurate records throughout each year that support the figures on your return and your audit should go smoothly. Finally, if the examiner's report shows that you owe additional tax, you will have thirty days to accept or contest the decision.

What You Can Do

The first step, of course, is to file your tax returns (or request for extensions), on or before the IRS deadline. If you are charged a penalty for filing late, send a notarized statement and whatever documentation you have showing the date it was mailed. If you are filing late, include a letter and available supporting evidence explaining why. The IRS examiner may accept the late filing without a penalty.

Even if you have met the deadlines, it may not be enough. The IRS can come back to you for more money. This is done by sending you a letter stating that there is a deficiency in your tax payment.

- If you dispute a calculation, send a letter of explanation, including your calculation. Keep your letter short, simple, and to the point so it can be easily understood. (See page 85 for a sample letter.) The IRS notices usually come in duplicate, giving you the copy to use for your response. You should include this copy, and always reference the IRS file number on your correspondence to make sure it does not get lost. You should send correspondence by certified mail, with a return receipt requested. This way, there can be no dispute by the IRS that they received your response.

- If you get further notices without any acknowledgment of the letter you sent, write again and include copies of all correspondence you already sent regarding that particular claim. If you still get another notice, contact the IRS Problem Resolution Officer nearest you. If you believe the IRS is beyond the time limitation, you can file a petition in the U.S. Tax Court to have the taxes, interest and penalties dropped. (See page 86 for a sample petition.)

- If you owe the bill, negotiate with the IRS for a reduced lump-sum amount *or* arrange a payment plan. If you do set up a payment plan, make sure you keep the payments current. If you do not, the IRS can take other actions to collect.

- Consider taking out a loan from your bank or other source, if possible, and paying the IRS off. It may be better to owe money to the bank than to risk your house being seized by the IRS. This would also eliminate the IRS charge for penalties and interest. (If the IRS has waived penalties, or none are being charged, then a payment plan with the IRS might make better economic sense.)

- Finally, a bankruptcy filing will temporarily stop all actions by the IRS to collect unpaid taxes. However, bankruptcy will not discharge your debt to the IRS (unless the time limitation has expired *and* you have not had negotiations with the IRS or a tax court case determination within 240 days of filing the bankruptcy petition). A Chapter 13 filing will not discharge the debt for unpaid taxes, but will allow you to pay the entire amount due according to your repayment plan schedule set up through the bankruptcy procedure.

FOR FURTHER RESEARCH

The IRS list of exemptions is found in United States Code Title 12, Chapter 64, Subtitle F-Collection, Section 6334. A list of IRS publications is available at **http://www.irs.ustreas.gov/forms_pubs**. The text of these publications is available either by mail, or directly on the website. IRS Publication 1 explains your rights as a taxpayer, including your rights to taxpayer assistance.

The Internal Revenue Service also provides information by telephone (800-829-1040), and forms by calling 800-829-3676. The general website is

http://www.irs.ustreas.gov

SAMPLE IRS CORRESPONDENCE

September 20, 2001

Internal Revenue Service   CERTIFIED MAIL
Atlanta, GA 39901   RETURN RECEIPT REQUESTED
P-288-398-487

RE: Jane Doe
Social Security No. 555-55-5555
Your file reference no.95-34453

Dear Sir or Madam,

I have received your letter of September 10, 2001, a copy of which is attached, advising me that I still owe $759.28.

I have recalculated my 1997 tax return and come up with the same figures as before. My calculations are attached.

Please correct your records and stop sending me notices, or explain specifically where and how the error is to be found.

Thank you.

Sincerely,

Jane Doe

This letter should be sent in response to a notice of deficiency or a correction notice.

SAMPLE TAX CASE PETITION FORM

PETITION
(SMALL TAX CASE)
UNITED STATES TAX COURT

Jane Doe,	)
Petitioner,	)
	)
vs.	) Docket No. _____
	)
Commissioner of Internal Revenue,	)
Respondent.	)

PETITION

1. Petitioner ask the Court to redetermine the tax deficiencies for the year <u>1997</u> as set forth in the Notice of Deficiency dated <u>September 10, 2001</u>, a copy of which is attached to this Petition. The Notice was issued by the Office of the Internal Revenue Service at <u>Atlanta, Georgia</u>.

2. Petitioner's taxpayer identification number (social security number) is <u>555-55-5555</u>.

3. Petitioner makes the following claim(s) regarding his/their tax liability:

Year	Amount of Deficiency Disputed	Addition to Tax (Penalty) Disputed	Amount of Over-payment Claim
1997	$759.28	$113.90	-0-

4. Those adjustments or changes in the Notice of Deficiency with which Petitioners disagrees and why: The IRS has failed to show where any errors were made in the Petitioner's tax return as originally filed.

Petitioner requests that the proceedings in this case be conducted as a "Small Tax Case" under Section 7463 of the Internal Revenue Code of 1954, as amended, and Rule 172 of the Rules of Practice and Procedure of the United States Tax Court. A decision in a "Small Tax Case" is final and cannot be appealed by either party.

_____
Signature of Petitioner
447 Tea Party Lane
Clearwater, FL 33760
(813) 555-5555

LOAN DISCLOSURE REQUIREMENTS— TRUTH IN LENDING 7

THE FEDERAL LAW

Although the text of the Federal Consumer Credit Act, which includes the Consumer Credit Cost Disclosure requirements, is too extensive and complex to recite in this book, it is important for you to know that you have the right to certain information about a loan given to you by a lender or creditor.

Congress established the cost disclosure requirements to assure that every creditor who, in the ordinary course of business, regularly extends, offers to extend, or arranges, for the extension of consumer credit, gives meaningful information regarding the cost of the credit and other relevant information. This is so that you may readily compare the various credit terms available to you from different sources and avoid the uninformed use of credit.

You should have the benefit of sufficient information about the proposed loan so that you can make an informed decision as to whether you want to accept the terms. If you have not had the benefit of all the information that the law requires the creditor give you, then you may have the basis for a lawsuit against the creditor. Or, you may have a counterclaim if the creditor sues you for non-payment.

The Truth in Lending regulations (also known as *Regulation Z*), set forth the rules lenders must comply with when they give you credit. (Code of Federal Regulations, Title 12, Chapter II, Part 226.) It gives you the right to cancel certain credit transactions which involve a lien on your residence. It also gives you certain legal rights if the lender has misrepresented a loan to you, or has failed to make all the disclosures accurately as required under the law. (The Consumer Credit Act requires disclosure in other consumer credit transactions, as well as leases and credit cards, which are discussed in Chapters 8 and 9.)

REQUIRED DISCLOSURES

The disclosures that must be made by a lender include:

- the identity of the creditor (lender);
- the amount financed, which is the amount of credit of which the borrower has actual use;
- along with the disclosure of the amount financed, a statement of your right to obtain, upon a written request, a written itemization of the amount financed (which must then be furnished);
- the finance charge;
- the finance charge expressed as an annual percentage rate;
- the number, amount, and due dates or period of payments scheduled to repay the total loan;

- (where the lender is also the seller), the total of the cash price of the property and the finance charge;
- descriptive explanations of the terms:
  - amount financed,
  - finance charge,
  - annual percentage rate,
  - total of payments, and
  - total sale price.

NOTE: *The descriptive explanation of total sale price must include a reference to the amount of the down payment;*

- where credit is secured, as with a mortgage, a statement that a security interest has been taken in either (a) the property that is purchased as part of the credit transaction, or (b) property not purchased as part of the credit transaction identified by item or type;
- any dollar charge or percentage amount that may be imposed by a creditor solely on account of a late payment, other than a deferral or extension charge;
- a statement as to whether or not you are entitled to a rebate of any finance charge upon refinancing or prepayment in full, if the obligation involves a precomputed finance charge. A statement whether or not there will be a penalty imposed in those same circumstances if the obligation involves a finance charge computed from time to time by application of a rate to the unpaid principal balance;
- a statement that you should refer to the appropriate contract document for any information that document provides

about nonpayment, default, the right to accelerate the maturity of the debt, and prepayment rebates and penalties;

- in any residential mortgage transaction, a statement indicating whether someone who buys the property from you may assume the debt obligation on its original terms and conditions;

- any variable rate information;

- information about a demand feature of the financing (when payment can be demanded by creditor);

- creditor's late payment policy;

- information about any security interest the creditor is taking and related charges;

- insurance requirements; and

- required deposit information.

Errors by the creditor in the Truth in Lending Disclosures are usually not brought to the creditor's attention by the borrower until the creditor tries to collect the debt. If the creditor finds an error before any default in payment, the creditor will probably prepare new documents with the correct information.

LOAN REQUESTS — TIME PERIODS IN WHICH DISCLOSURES MUST BE MADE

Lenders are required to provide you with specific information about the terms of financing within certain prescribed time periods, as follows.

Telephone Orders

You may place a purchase order by mail or telephone without being personally solicited by the creditor. The cash price and total sale price and the terms of financing, including the annual percentage rate, are set forth in the creditor's catalog, or other printed material distributed to the public. The required disclosures may be made by the creditor at any time earlier than the first payment due date.

Loan Requests by Telephone

You may make a request for a loan by mail or telephone even when the creditor has not personally solicited you. The terms of financing, including the annual percentage rate for representative amounts of credit, are set forth in the creditor's printed material distributed to the public, in the loan contract, or other printed material delivered to you. Then, the disclosures must be made no later than the date the first payment is due.

If the creditor personally solicits you in either case, the disclosures must be made *before* you obligate yourself to the creditor.

Purchasing in a Series

Your purchase may be one of a series according to an agreement providing that the deferred payment price of a particular sale be added to the existing outstanding balance. If you have already agreed to the annual percentage rate and finance charge, and the creditor is not retaining a security interest in any of the property you have purchased, then the disclosure may be made any time before the first payment is due.

NOTE: *See also "Good Faith Estimate—Residential Mortgages" on page 106.*

FINANCE CHARGE AND
ANNUAL PERCENTAGE RATE (APR)

Regulation Z spells out exactly how the finance charge and annual percentage rate on your loan are to be determined, and how these and other charges related to your loan are to be disclosed to you. The manner in which these calculations are made is determined by federal statute regulation and by the Board of Governors of the Federal Reserve System ("Board").

Finance Charge

In determining whether a lender has given you all the required information about your loan, one of the most important items to review is the finance charge. The *finance charge* is determined as the sum of all charges, payable directly or indirectly by the borrower, and imposed directly or indirectly by the creditor as an incident to the extension of credit. The following charges are examples of costs included in the finance charge:

- interest and any amount payable under a point, discount, or other system of additional charges;

- service or carrying charge;

- loan fee, finder's fee, or similar charge;

- fee for an investigation or credit report; or

- premium or other charge for any guarantee or insurance protecting the creditor against the obligor's default or other credit loss.

Example: A buyer of a food freezer was required to purchase a freezer service policy to assure repair of the freezer for the duration of the period the buyer agreed to make installment payments. The charge for the service policy was added to the sale price and included in the amount financed, but not disclosed to the buyer. The cost of the freezer service policy was a finance charge, the disclosure of which was required by law. The seller was liable for damages to the buyer.

In deciding whether an item must be included in the finance charge, the important question is whether the lender refuses to extend credit until you agree to pay the charge. If a charge is not itemized and disclosed by the lender, it still needs to be included in the computation of the finance charge, even if the charge is not a charge for credit.

Annual Percentage Rate (APR)

The APR simply reflects the cost of your loan as a yearly rate. This figure must be disclosed to you, because it will usually be higher than the interest rate you are paying on your note. Borrowers often wonder whether the bank has increased the interest rate quoted to them. The difference between the interest rate quoted and stated on your promissory note and the interest rate (APR) shown on the disclosure form is due to difference in calculations.

There are several methods of determining the annual percentage rate (APR) applied to your loan. The most important point to remember is that any prepaid finance charges are considered a reduction in the *principal* amount of the loan.

Example: If you borrow $10,000.00 at 10% interest for one year, and the bank deducts $300.00 in loan closing costs from the $10,000.00 and you must make up the difference, then you have actually only received $9,700.00. The total of 10% interest on $10,000.00, or $1,000.00, is $11,000.00. This is the amount you will pay according to your loan. However, because of the deduction of closing costs, the bank is actually giving you only $9,700.00. The total of $11,000.00 you will pay ($10,000 plus $1,000 interest) is actually $9,700.00 (the $10,000 less $300 in charges) at 13.40% interest.

Remember that any income the bank earns as the result of your loan is considered a finance charge, including a bank appraisal fee, document preparation fee, points, origination fee, etc. These charges should be considered a reduction in the principal amount of the loan.

The lender will take three variables into consideration in computing the APR:

1) the number of payments to be made over the complete term of the loan (usually 360 for a real estate loan);

2) the interest rate; and

3) the principal balance remaining to be paid on the loan after deducting those items that are prepaid finance charges.

The fourth variable, the total of the periodic (monthly) payments (principal and interest), will then be computed.

A rough approximation of the calculation is as follows:

- first the finance charge to be paid over the term of the loan is totalled (in a real estate loan, the monthly finance charge will vary according to an amortization schedule);

- second, this total is then divided by the number of years of the loan; and

- third, this figure is then again divided by the total amount financed (including the principal amount of the loan and reflecting any finance charges).

NOTE: *This is a complicated calculation, and is not to be attempted arithmetically, but should be reviewed by someone competent and experienced in applying the Regulation Z requirements.*

An APR on an open-end (equity line) loan is calculated as if the loan were carried out to full term at the highest interest rate.

All items required to be disclosed must be disclosed clearly, conspicuously, and in meaningful sequence. The terms "annual percentage rate" and "finance charge" must be disclosed more conspicuously than other terms or information provided in connection with a transaction, except information relating the identity of the creditor. The disclosures must be made to the person who is to be obligated on the loan. (If you are taking out the loan, with your father's advice, then the disclosures must be made to you—making them to your father is not sufficient.)

TRUTH IN LENDING DISCLOSURE STATEMENT

A sample Truth in Lending Disclosure Statement is on page 105. The box titled "Annual Percentage Rate" may be different from the rate quoted to you at the time of your mortgage application, and may be different from the interest rate you were promised. This rate should reflect any prepaid costs or items included in the financing.

Example: The rate shown is 9.65%. The rate the borrower is paying on an $80,000.00 loan is 9.25%. The promissory note will show $80,000.00 to be paid back at 9.25% interest. Take the $80,000.00, less $2,728.00 in total closing costs (these include $800 in origination fee, $1600 discount points, $113 appraisal fee, $50 credit report, and $165 underwriting fee). The $77,272.00, with the payments calculated on the $80,000.00 amount (since $80,000 includes the amount paid on behalf of and given to the borrower), comes to 9.65% annual percentage rate.

The box titled "Finance Charge" shows the total amount of interest you will be paying over the total term of the loan.

The box titled "Amount Financed" is somewhat less than the amount of the mortgage because the prepaid costs have been deducted, as described above.

The box titled "Total of Payments" is the total of the figures in the previous two boxes, representing the total amount that you will be paying if you pay the full term of the loan.

NOTE: *Although beyond the scope of this book, you should also note that banks and other real estate lenders are required to follow the Federal Real Estate Settlement Procedures Act of 1974 (RESPA) which regulates settlement of a residential loan transaction. For information about RESPA, write to:*

> U.S. Department of Housing and Urban Development
> Director, Office of Insured Single Family Housing
> Attention: RESPA
> 451 Seventh St., S.W,
> Washington, D.C. 20410
> 202-708-1112

For information regarding manufactured home financing requirements, contact:

> Office of Manufactured Housing and Regulatory Functions
> 451 Seventh Street S.W.
> Washington, D.C. 20410

GOOD FAITH ESTIMATE— RESIDENTIAL MORTGAGES

In a residential mortgage transaction, the lender must make a *good faith* (reasonable and as accurate as possible) estimate of the disclosures required under Regulation Z *before* the credit is extended, or the lender must either deliver or place the estimate in the mail to the borrower *no later than three business days* after the lender receives the borrower's written application, whichever date is earlier. If the good faith estimate contains an annual percentage rate that is subsequently determined to be inaccurate by the acceptable calculations, then the lender must furnish another good faith estimate at the time of settlement (when the loan is actually made and documents signed). (See page 106 for sample of Good Faith Estimate.)

EQUITY LINE MORTGAGES AND YOUR RIGHT TO RESCIND

If you have borrowed funds for purposes other than the purchase of your principal residence, and the lender has taken an interest in your residence as collateral for the loan, the law requires that you be given a three-day *right of rescission*. In other words, you have until midnight of the third business day, following the date of signing the loan documents or receipt of the all required disclosures, to cancel the loan. However, you must notify the creditor by mail, telegram, or other writing of your cancellation.

Every joint owner who will be obligated to pay back the loan has the right to receive the disclosures and must be given a notice of the right to cancel. (See page 108 for a sample notice.)

Release from Your Obligations

When you exercise your right to rescind, you are not liable for any finance or other charge, and any security interest the creditor may have in your property becomes void. Within twenty days after you exercise your right to rescind, the creditor must return to you any money or property given as earnest money, down payment, or otherwise, and must take any action required to reflect the termination of any security interest the creditor may have acquired as a result of the transaction.

Property to Be Returned to Creditor

As the borrower you must also return to the creditor, within a reasonable time period after you rescind the transaction, any funds or value the creditor has advanced to you. However, if the creditor fails to return the property required to be returned to you, then you have no further obligation to return the funds to the creditor.

If the Creditor Fails to Take the Property

If the creditor does not take possession of the property within ten days of the date you offer, you may be entitled to keep the property. (In most cases this would involve a return of the principal amount loaned to you by the creditor.) A court can refuse your request to have the transaction rescinded if you fail to return any loan proceeds advanced to you by the lender.

Loans Not Affected by Right of Rescission

The right of rescission does not apply to:

- a *residential mortgage transaction* when the funds are used to purchase the property;

- a transaction that constitutes the refinancing or consolidation (with no new advances) of the principal balance then due and any accrued and unpaid finance charges of an existing extension of credit by the same creditor, secured by an interest in the same property;

- a transaction when an agency of a state is a creditor; or

- advances under a preexisting open-end credit plan if a security interest has already been retained or acquired by the

99

lender and such advances are in accordance with a previously established credit limit for such plan.

If the lender fails to provide you with the information required to be disclosed, you have three years from the date of the conclusion of the transaction, or when you sell the property, whichever comes first, to rescind the transaction. If the creditor fails to disclose required information, you are not limited by the normal three-day rescission period.

Balloon Payments on Consumer Loans

Some states prohibit balloon payments on consumer loans for family or household purposes; others require that you be given the right to refinance the loan when the balloon payment comes due. (A *balloon payment* is the amount due at the end of a loan term after you have made regular, smaller payments for a period of time.) Your state attorney general's office or the consumer office should have information regarding balloon payments on consumer loans.

Refinancing

If any existing extension of credit is refinanced, two or more existing extensions of credit are consolidated, or an existing obligation is increased, these will be considered new transactions subject to the disclosure requirements of the Act. If your loan has been refinanced or the terms have otherwise changed, determine whether your lender gave you all the required information.

When Disclosure Is Not Required

The disclosure requirements described above do not apply to the following transactions:

- credit transactions involving extensions of credit primarily for business, commercial, or agricultural purposes, or to government or governmental agencies, or to organizations;

- transactions in securities or commodities accounts by a broker-dealer registered with the Securities and Exchange Commission;

- credit transactions, other than those in which a security interest is or will be acquired in *real property*, or in *personal property* used or expected to be used as the principal dwelling of the consumer, in which the total amount financed exceeds $25,000.00; or

- transactions under public utility tariffs, if the Board determines that a State regulatory body regulates the charges for the public utility services involved, the charges for delayed payment, and any discount allowed for early payment.

The numerous laws and regulations under the Consumer Credit Act cover consumer credit transactions primarily for personal, family, household, or agricultural purposes.

Lenders' Liabilities And Your Rights And Obligations

The creditor has no liability if, within sixty days of discovering an error and before receiving notice from you of the error, the creditor notifies you and makes the appropriate adjustments.

The creditor makes sure that you will not be required to pay an amount greater than the charge actually disclosed, or the dollar equivalent of the annual percentage rate actually disclosed, whichever is lower.

The creditor will not be held liable if the creditor shows that the violation was not intentional and resulted from an honest error, including clerical or computer malfunction. However, an error of legal judgment with respect to a person's obligations is not considered an honest error. In most real estate loan transactions with a commercial lender you will be asked to sign a document that says you agree to cooperate if a correction is required due to a clerical error. (See page 107 for a sample compliance agreement.)

You have no legal right to offset any amount that the creditor may owe you against any other amount you owe the creditor, unless you have a court judgment against the creditor. However, you should assert the creditor's violation of the Consumer Credit Act as a defense against any legal action to collect a debt brought by a creditor who is in violation of the Act.

NOTE: *In a real estate foreclosure action, Regulation Z may be your strongest defense.*

Considering the volume of paperwork required in a loan transaction and the number of transactions a commercial lender may make, it is possible that an error was made. You should get a copy of all the disclosure documents related to your loan. You should then review them carefully with someone who fully understands the disclosure requirements and the calculations. If there is a possibility of an error, it may be wise for you to hire an attorney to review the documents and give you an opinion as to whether you should proceed legally against the lender. (Even if ultimately the court does not agree that the lender violated the Consumer Credit Act, using this as a defense will delay the lender's lawsuit, including a foreclosure action.) Remember that, if you are successful in a lawsuit against a creditor who violated any provisions of the Consumer Credit Act, your attorneys fees and costs must be paid by the creditor.

For any violation of the Consumer Credit Act, a creditor may be liable to you in an amount equal to:

- any actual damage suffered by you as a result of the failure to disclose all of the information required;

- twice the amount of any finance charge in connection with the transaction; or

- the reasonable attorneys fees and costs incurred in a successful legal action.

FOR FURTHER RESEARCH

If you need additional information regarding Regulation Z, you may write to:

> Division of Consumer and Community Affairs
> Board of Governors of the Federal Reserve System
> Washington, D.C. 20551

Or write to your regional Federal Trade Commission office, Division of Credit Practices-Bureau of Consumer Affairs. (See Appendix C.) The text of the Act is contained in United States

Code, Title 15, Chapter 41, Subchapter I, Consumer Credit Cost Disclosure, Sections 1601 through 1635. The regulations enforcing the laws are found in the Code of Federal Regulations "Truth in Lending Regulations," Banks & Banking, Title 12, Part 226.

SAMPLE TRUTH IN LENDING DISCLOSURE STATEMENT

TRUTH IN LENDING DISCLOSURE STATEMENT

Creditor	Applicant(s)
Mailing Address	Property Address
Loan Number	Preparation Date

ANNUAL PERCENTAGE RATE	FINANCE CHARGE	Amount Financed	Total of Payments
The cost of your credit as a yearly rate.	The dollar amount the credit will cost you.	The amount of credit provided to you or on your behalf.	The amount you will have paid after you have made all payments as scheduled.
E 9.65 %	E$ 159,658.72	E$ 77,272.00	E$ 236,930.72

PAYMENT SCHEDULE:

NUMBER OF PAYMENTS	* AMOUNT OF PAYMENTS	MONTHLY PAYMENTS ARE DUE BEGINNING	NUMBER OF PAYMENTS	* AMOUNT OF PAYMENTS	MONTHLY PAYMENTS ARE DUE BEGINNING

* Includes mortgage insurance premiums, excludes taxes, hazard insurance or flood insurance.

DEMAND FEATURE: ☐ This loan does not have a Demand Feature ☐ This loan has a Demand Feature.

ITEMIZATION: You have a right at this time to an ITEMIZATION OF AMOUNT FINANCED.
I/We ☐ do ☐ do not want an itemization.

REQUIRED DEPOSIT:
☐ The annual percentage rate does not take into account your required deposit.

VARIABLE RATE FEATURE:
☐ This Loan has a Variable Rate Feature. Variable Rate Disclosures have been provided to you earlier.

SECURITY: You are giving a security interest in:

ASSUMPTION: Someone buying this property
☐ cannot assume the remaining balance due under original mortgage terms.
☐ may assume, subject to lender's conditions, the remaining balance due under original mortgage terms.

FILING / RECORDING FEES: $

PROPERTY INSURANCE:
☐ Property / hazard insurance is a required condition of this loan. Borrower may purchase this insurance from any insurance company acceptable to the lender.
Hazard insurance ☐ is ☐ is not available through the lender at an estimated cost of   for a   month term.

LATE CHARGES: If your payment is more than   days late, you will be charged a late charge of   % of the overdue payment.

PREPAYMENT: If you prepay this loan in full or in part, you
☐ may ☐ will not have to pay a penalty.
☐ may ☐ will not be entitled to a refund of part of the finance charge.

See your contract documents for any additional information regarding non-payment, default, required repayment in full before scheduled date, and payment refunds and penalties.
E means estimate.

I/We hereby acknowledge reading and receiving a complete copy of this disclosure. I/We understand there is no commitment for the creditor to make this loan and there is no obligation for me/us to accept this loan upon delivery or signing of this disclosure.

_____ Date   _____ Date

_____ Date   _____ Date

GENESIS 2000, INC. * V9.3/W11.0 * (818) 223-3260   Form RegZD (03/95)

SAMPLE GOOD FAITH ESTIMATE

GOOD FAITH ESTIMATE

Lender:	Sales Price:
Address:	Base Loan Amount:
	Total Loan Amount:
Applicant(s):	Interest Rate:
	Type of Loan:
Property Address:	Preparation Date:
	Loan Number:

The information provided below reflects estimates of the charges which you are likely to incur at the settlement of your loan. The fees listed are estimates - actual charges may be more or less. Your transaction may not involve a fee for every item listed. The numbers listed beside the estimates generally correspond to the numbered lines contained in the HUD-1 or HUD-1A settlement statement which you will be receiving at settlement. The HUD-1 or HUD-1A settlement statement will show you the actual cost for items paid at settlement.

800	ITEMS PAYABLE IN CONNECTION WITH LOAN:			1100	TITLE CHARGES:	
801	Origination Fee @	% + $	$	1101	Closing or Escrow Fee	$
802	Discount Fee @	% + $	$	1102	Abstract or Title Search	$
803	Appraisal Fee		$	1103	Title Examination	$
804	Credit Report		$	1105	Document Preparation Fee	$
805	Lender's Inspection Fee		$	1106	Notary Fee	$
806	Mortgage Insurance Application Fee		$	1107	Attorney's Fee	$
807	Assumption Fee		$	1108	Title Insurance	$
808	Mortgage Broker Fee		$			$
810	Tax Related Service Fee		$			$
811	Application Fee		$			$
812	Commitment Fee		$			$
813	Lender's Rate Lock-In Fee		$			$
814	Processing Fee		$			$
815	Underwriting Fee		$	1200	GOVERNMENT RECORDING AND TRANSFER CHARGES:	
816	Wire Transfer Fee		$	1201	Recording Fee	$
			$	1202	City/County Tax/Stamps	$
900	ITEMS REQUIRED BY LENDER TO BE PAID IN ADVANCE:			1203	State Tax/Stamps	$
901	Interest for days @ $ /day		$	1204	Intangible Tax	$
902	Mortgage Insurance Premium		$			$
903	Hazard Insurance Premium		$			$
904	County Property Taxes		$			$
905	Flood Insurance		$			$
			$	1300	ADDITIONAL SETTLEMENT CHARGES:	
				1301	Survey	$
1000	RESERVES DEPOSITED WITH LENDER:			1302	Pest Inspection	$
1001	Hazard Ins. Mo. @$ Per Mo.		$			$
1002	Mortgage Ins. Mo. @$ Per Mo.		$			$
1004	Tax & Assmt. Mo. @$ Per Mo.		$			$
1006	Flood Insurance		$			$
			$		TOTAL ESTIMATED SETTLEMENT CHARGES:	$

"S"/"B" designates those costs to be paid by Seller/Broker.
"A" designates those costs affecting APR.

TOTAL ESTIMATED MONTHLY PAYMENT:			TOTAL ESTIMATED FUNDS NEEDED TO CLOSE:	
Principal & Interest	$			
Real Estate Taxes	$			
Hazard Insurance	$	Down Payment	$	
Flood Insurance	$	Estimated Closing Costs	$	
Mortgage Insurance	$	Estimated Prepaid Items / Reserves	$	
Other	$	Total Paid Items (Subtract)	$	
TOTAL MONTHLY PAYMENT	$	Other	$	
		CASH FROM BORROWER	$	

THIS SECTION IS COMPLETED ONLY IF A PARTICULAR PROVIDER OF SERVICE IS REQUIRED. Listed below are providers of service which we required you to use. The charges indicated in the Good Faith Estimate above are based upon the corresponding charge of the below designated providers.

ITEM NO.	NAME & ADDRESS OF PROVIDER	TELEPHONE NO.	NATURE OF RELATIONSHIP

These estimates are provided pursuant to the Real Estate Settlement Procedures Act of 1974, as amended (RESPA). Additional information can be found in the HUD Special Information Booklet, which is to be provided to you by your mortgage broker or lender, if your application is to purchase residential property and the Lender will take a first lien on the property.

Applicant	Date	Applicant	Date
Applicant	Date	Applicant	Date

☐ This Good Faith Estimate is being provided by a mortgage broker, and no lender has yet been obtained.

SAMPLE COMPLIANCE AGREEMENT

LENDER:
BORROWER(S):

PROPERTY ADDRESS:
LOAN NO.:

ERROR AND OMISSIONS/COMPLIANCE AGREEMENT

STATE OF
COUNTY OF

The undersigned borrower(s) for an in consideration of the above-referenced Lender funding the closing of this loan agrees, if requested by Lender or Closing Agent for Lender, to fully cooperate and adjust for clerical errors, any or all loan closing documentation if deemed necessary or desirable in the reasonable discretion of Lender to enable Lender to Mortgage Association, Federal Home Loan Mortgage Corporation, Government National Mortgage Association, Federal Housing Authority or the Department of Veterans Affairs, or any Municipal Bonding Authority.

The undersigned borrower(s) agree(s) to comply with all above noted requests by the above-referenced Lender within 20 days from date of mailing of said requests. Borrower(s) agree(s) to assume all costs including, by way of illustration and not limitation, actual expenses, legal fees and marketing losses for failing to comply with correction requests in the above noted time period.

The undersigned borrower(s) do hereby so agree and covenant in order to assure that this loan documentation executed this date will conform and be acceptable in the marketplace in the instance of transfer, sale or conveyance by Lender of its interest in and to said loan documentation, and to assure marketable title in the said borrower(s).

DATED effective this day of

_____   _____
(Borrower)   (Borrower)

_____   _____
(Borrower)   (Borrower)

Sworn to and subscribed before me this day of

_____
(Notary Public)

My Commission Expires:

SAMPLE NOTICE OF RIGHT TO CANCEL

Loan No.

NOTICE OF RIGHT TO CANCEL

Your Right to Cancel

You are entering into a transaction that will result in a mortgage on your home. You have a legal right under Federal law to cancel this transaction, without cost, within three business days from whichever of the following events occurs last:

(1) The date of the transaction, which is June 11, 2001; or

(2) The date you received your Truth in Lending disclosures; or

(3) The date you received this notice of your right to cancel.

If you cancel the transaction, the mortgage is also canceled. Within 20 calendar days after we receive your notice, we must take the steps necessary to reflect the fact that the mortgage on your home has been canceled, and we must return to you any money or property you have given to us or to anyone else in connection with this transaction.

You may keep any money or property we have given you until we have done the things mentioned above, but you must then offer to return the money or property. If it is impractical or unfair for you to return the property, you must offer its reasonable value. You may offer to return the property at your home or at the location of the property. They money must be returned to the address below. If we do not take possession of the money or property within 20 calendar days of your offer, you may keep it without further obligations.

How to Cancel

If you decide to cancel this transaction, you may do so by notifying us in writing, at Yourbank, Anywhere,USA.

You may use any written statement that is signed and dated by you and states your intention to cancel, or you may use this notice by dating and signing below. Keep one copy of this Notice because it contains important information about your rights.

If you cancel by mail or telegram, you must send the notice no later than midnight of June 14, 2001 (or midnight of the third business days following the latest of the three events listed above). If you send or deliver your written notice to cancel some other way, it must be delivered to the above address no later than that time.

I WISH TO CANCEL

_____   _____
Customer's Signature   Date

CREDIT CARDS AND OTHER *OPEN-END* CONSUMER CREDIT LOANS 8

OPEN-END CREDIT

An *open-end* credit plan is when the creditor reasonably expects repeated transactions, prescribes the terms of the transactions, and provides for a finance charge that may be computed from time to time on the outstanding unpaid balance. A credit card account and a credit line are examples of open-end credit plans. A credit card is in reality a loan from a lending institution that pays the merchant within a few days of receiving the loan document (credit card receipt) from the merchant. The lending institution (credit card issuer) then sends you an invoice.

Becoming eligible for a credit card depends upon having a solid credit history—or at least it should. These days, a lot of companies are fairly free and easy about giving consumers cards. More than ever, consumers need to rely on their own financial common sense to sift out the genuine good deals, and not to overindulge and sink into deep credit card debt.

INFORMATION THAT MUST BE DISCLOSED

Before opening any account under an open-end consumer credit plan, the creditor must disclose to you each of the following items, to the extent they apply to your situation:

- the conditions under which a finance charge may be imposed, including the time period (if any) within which any credit extended may be repaid without incurring a finance charge (except that the creditor may, at his election and without disclosure, impose no finance charge if payment is received after the termination of the time period.) If no time period is provided for repayment, the creditor must disclose this fact;

- the method of determining the balance upon which a finance charge will be imposed;

- the method of determining the amount of the finance charge, including any minimum or fixed amount imposed as a finance charge;

- where one or more periodic rates (different rates in different time periods) may be used to compute the finance charge, each rate, the range of balances to which it applies, and the corresponding nominal annual percentage rate determined by multiplying the periodic rate by the number of periods in a year;

- identification of other charges that may be imposed as part of the plan, and their method of computation;

- in cases where the credit is or will be secured, a statement that a security interest has been or will be taken in (a) the property purchased as part of the credit transaction, or (b) property not purchased as part of the credit transaction identified by item or type.

Example: Before opening an account under an open-end credit plan, the seller only said that it might, at its option, retain a security interest in merchandise at the time the purchaser bought merchandise. The seller failed to specifically disclose the conditions under which it would retain or acquire any security interest. The failure to disclose was a violation of this section. (Under federal law, a creditor is not allowed to take the following items as collateral unless the loan is being made for the purchase of the items: clothing, furniture, appliances, linens, china, kitchenware, television, wedding rings, and other personal effects.); and

- a statement of the protection provided as to the creditor's and your responsibilities. With respect to one billing cycle per calendar year, at intervals between six months and eighteen months, the creditor must send a statement to each borrower to whom the creditor is required to send a statement that contains the information as described in the next section.

Since the purpose of this law is to permit informed credit shopping, the required disclosures should be made *before* a credit transaction is completed.

BILLING DISCLOSURE REQUIREMENTS

After the credit is extended, your creditor will send you statements. In each billing cycle your creditor is required to send you certain information, including:

- the outstanding balance in the account at the beginning of the statement period;
- the amount, date, and a brief description of each extension of credit during the billing period;
- the total amount credited to the account during the period;
- the amount of any finance charge added to the bill during the period;

- if more than one rate is used (for example, a cash advance often accrues a different interest rate from credit card purchases), the breakdown of the charges;
- the total finance charge billed as an annual percentage rate;
- the balance on which the finance charge was computed and a statement of how the balance was determined;
- the outstanding balance in the account at the end of the period;
- the date payment must be made by in order to avoid additional finance charges; and
- the address you are making inquiries to about your billing.

PENALTIES FOR VIOLATIONS

The penalties for violating any of the above requirements are the same as for failure to comply with disclosure requirements for credit as listed in Chapter 7:

- any actual damage sustained by the borrower as a result of the failure;
- twice the amount of any finance charge in connection with the transaction between $100 and $1,000; and
- the reasonable attorneys fees and costs incurred in a successful legal action.

CONSUMER LOAN BILLING PROCEDURES

Billing for consumer loan payments is regulated by the Fair Credit Billing Act (FCBA) (Public Law 93-495). If a bill is incorrect, you should notify the creditor, in writing by certified mail, return receipt requested, within sixty days after the creditor sent you the bill. The notice to the creditor should state your name and account number, that you believe the bill to be incorrect, and your reasons why. (See page 116 for a sample letter.) Unless the creditor then hears from you otherwise, the creditor has thirty days after receiving your letter of dispute to send you written acknowledgment of your dispute. Within two billing cycles after that (no more than ninety days), the creditor must make appropriate corrections on your bill, notify you of the corrections, or must make an investigation.

If the creditor's investigation shows that the amount is correct, then the creditor must send you a written explanation, along with any supporting documents. If you have disputed the bill based upon the fact that you have been charged for goods that were never delivered to you, then the creditor should delete the charge unless it is determined that the goods were actually delivered, mailed, or otherwise sent to you. The creditor must have a statement showing that fact.

A creditor who does not follow the rules under this law forfeits any right to collect from you the amount you have disputed and any finance charge on that amount (total not to exceed $50.00).

After the creditor has received notice from you under the FCBA, the creditor may not threaten to report adversely to anyone about your credit standing because of your failure to pay the disputed amount, nor may any legal action be taken to collect the amount. You cannot be denied credit because you have disputed a bill.

UNSOLICITED CREDIT CARDS

The law provides that "no credit card shall be issued except in response to a request or application therefor." (This does not apply to renewal of, or substitution for, a credit card that you previously accepted.) If you receive a credit card without applying for it, the issuing company is fully responsible for its use. However, if you sign the card, use it or notify the company that you will keep it, then in many states you have "accepted" the card and will be liable for charges.

LOST OR STOLEN CREDIT CARD

As the holder of a credit card, you will be liable for the unauthorized use of that card only if:

- the card is an accepted credit card;
- the liability is less than $50.00;
- the card issuer gives adequate notice to you of your potential liability;
- the card issuer has given you a description of how to notify the card issuer of a loss or theft (this can be printed on the billing statement);
- the unauthorized use is before the card issuer has been notified that an unauthorized use has occurred or may occur as a result of loss or theft; and
- the card issuer has provided a method whereby you can be identified as the person authorized to use the card.

In order to hold you liable, the card issuer must prove that the use was authorized, or that there are valid reasons for holding you liable.

NOTE: *if you allow someone else to use your card, even if you limit the amount charged and the limit is exceeded, this is not considered unauthorized use.*

114

NEW CREDIT CARD FRAUD

Credit card fraud appears to be rampant. Be sure to *always* sign the back of your credit card. Be very careful about giving out your credit card expiration date and number, because once this information becomes available to others, almost anything can be purchased with your card and new accounts can be opened in your name.

The Internet is now a location for credit card fraud. Although efforts are being made by credit card companies to combat fraud, such as scrambling card numbers, you should be extremely cautious in using credit cards on the Internet (or anywhere). You might not be aware that your credit card information has been used by someone else until you receive an invoice. Check your statements very carefully. Report the unauthorized use to your card provider immediately.

FOR FURTHER RESEARCH

The laws regarding open-end consumer credit plans are found in United States Code, Title 15, Chapter 41, Subchapter I, Sections 1637 through 1666(j); correction of billing errors is explained in Section 1666. Sample forms as prescribed by the Federal Trade Commission are found in United Stated Code Annotated, Title 15, and in the Code of Federal Regulations, Title 12, Appendix G.

You should also check the Federal Trade Commission website at:

http://www.ftc.gov/bcp/conline/pubs/credit/fcb.htm

or call toll free: 877-FTC-HELP

SAMPLE LETTER—
NOTIFICATION OF INCORRECT BILLING

August 23, 2001

VISA   CERTIFIED MAIL
213 Interest Street   RETURN RECEIPT REQUESTED
Sometown, Anystate 12045   P-396-388-492

    RE: Account No. 5555-5555-5555-5555
          Name   Jane Doe

Dear Sir or Madam:

This letter is to notify you of an error in my July, 2001 statement. The amount shown on the statement as being charged for prescriptions from Jake's Pharmacy is $114.00. The total cost of the prescriptions was actually $14.00.

According to the Credit Billing Act, you have 30 days to confirm that you have received this letter unless you correct the item before that time. You then have two billing cycles in which to investigate and either confirm the $114.00 amount or correct the billing.

Enclosed is a copy of my bill from Jake's Pharmacy. Thank you.

                    Sincerely,

                    Jane Doe
                    1423 Egypt Lane
                    Denver, CO 80034

CONSUMER LEASE DISCLOSURES 9

The types of disclosures that must be made in consumer leases are regulated by the following:

The Truth in Lending Act (TLA), which includes "Truth in Leasing" provisions, and Regulation M, adopted by the Federal Reserve Board, contain federal disclosure requirements pertaining to consumer leases and the Consumer Leasing Act of 1976 (Public Law 94-240). States also have laws regulating leasing, some specifically addressing automobile leasing.

CONSUMER LEASE GENERALLY

A *consumer lease*, as defined in the Act, is a contract for the use of personal property for more than four months, and for a total payment of no more than $25,000.00, primarily for personal, family, or household purposes. Most commonly leased items are automobiles and furniture.However, any property that is not real estate is included in the regulations. The *lessee* is the person who is offered a lease; the *lessor* is the person offering to lease or arranging to lease under a consumer lease. It makes no difference that the lessee has the option to purchase the property at the end of the lease term.

DISCLOSURE REQUIREMENTS

You may find an advertisement in the newspaper similar to the following "Drive a fully equipped automobile for $199 per month.*" The asterisk refers to lease disclosures in small print at the bottom of the ad, which you probably will not notice. The ad gets your attention, you visit the dealership, and the salesperson misleads you into thinking you are buying the car rather than leasing it. Worse yet, because it is such a good deal, you decide to trade in your fully paid-for car, but the dealer does not give you credit for its full value.

Before the lease transaction is completed, the lessor must provide you with certain information, set out clearly and accurately. This information includes:

- a brief description of the leased property;
- the amount of any payment required at the time the lease term begins;
- the amount payable by you for any fees, registration, certificate of title, or license fees or taxes;
- the amount of other charges payable by you, which are not included in the periodic payments.
- A description of the charges and that you will be liable for the difference, if any, between the anticipated *fair market value* of the leased property and its appraised actual value at the termination of the lease, if the lease includes such liability;

- a statement of the amount or method of determining the amount of any liabilities the lease imposes upon you at the end of the term and whether or not you have the option to purchase the leased property and at what price and time;

- a statement setting forth all express warranties and guarantees made by the manufacturer or lessor with respect to the leased property; and identifying the party responsible for maintaining or servicing the leased property together with a description of the responsibility;

- a description of the insurance paid for by you, or the insurance required of you, including the types and amounts of coverage and costs;

- a description of any security interest held or to be retained by the lessor in connection with the lease and a clear identification of the property to which the security interest relates;

- the number, amount, and due date or periods of payments under the lease and the total amount of such *periodic* payments;

- if the lease provides that you will be responsible for paying the anticipated fair market value of the property on expiration of the lease, the lessor must disclose the fair market value of the property at the beginning of the lease, the total cost of the lease at the time it terminates, and the difference between the two amounts; and

- a statement of the terms under which you can terminate the lease before the end of the lease term and the method of determining any penalty or other charge for delinquency, *default*, late payments, or early termination.

The disclosures can be made in the lease contract to be signed by you. Where the lessor may be unable to provide exact dollar amounts, estimates can be given.

An advertisement by a radio broadcast to aid, promote, or assist in consumer leasing must meet the above disclosure advertisements, state the number, amounts, due dates or periods of scheduled payments and the total payments, and provide a toll-free number for consumers to use. The telephone number must be available for at least ten days from the date of the broadcast.

RESIDUAL VALUE CALCULATION

The *residual value* is the agreed-upon amount which will represent the value of the property at the end of the lease. If your lease includes an estimated residual value of the property, the estimate must be a reasonable approximation of the anticipated actual *fair market value* of the property at the expiration of the lease. (The fair market value is what a willing buyer would expect to pay.) The estimated residual value may be considered unreasonable if it exceeds the actual value by more than three times a single monthly lease payment. (This does not take into consideration a situation where the property is damaged beyond reasonable wear and tear—the lessor may set standards for reasonable wear and tear.)

If the estimated residual value is greater than three times the actual value, this may also be considered as evidence that the lessor acted in bad faith, and in that case the lessor cannot collect the excess amount unless a court grants a judgment in favor of the lessor. Of course, you can make a final adjustment with the lessor regarding the excess residual after the termination of the lease.

If a lease has a residual value provision at the termination of the lease, you may, at your own expense, get a professional appraisal of the property by an independent third party agreeable to both the lessor and to you. The appraisal will then be binding on both parties.

LIABILITIES FOR VIOLATIONS

If a lessor has violated any of the requirements under the Consumer Leasing Act, the lessor may be subject to the following liabilities as under other disclosure requirements:

- any actual damage sustained by you as a result of the violation;
- twenty-five percent of the total amount of monthly payments under the lease, except that the liability under this provision will not be less than $100 or greater than $1,000.00; and
- your reasonable attorney's fees and costs incurred if your legal action is successful.

In a successful court action by a lessee, the lessor is required to pay the lessee's attorney's fees. For violations under the Consumer Leasing Act, a court action must be brought within one year of the termination of the lease agreement.

Any penalties or other charges provided for in the lease against the lessee must be reasonable in light of the actual harm caused to the lessor.

FOR FURTHER RESEARCH

The federal laws regarding consumer leases are found in United States Code, Title 15, Subchapter I, Part E, Sections 1667 through 1667(e). The regulations are found in Code of Federal Regulations, Title 12, Part 226, Truth in Lending, Section 226.15.

United States Code, Title 15, Section 1667 (c) addresses the liability of advertisers of consumer leases.

REAL ESTATE LOAN FORECLOSURES 10

MORTGAGES

A *mortgage* is a lien the bank or other lender has against your real property, or an interest your lender has in your real property, as security for the note you have signed to pay for the property. (*Real property* refers to real estate; *personal property* usually refers to any other type of property.) Your mortgage is probably your largest debt, and you may need to make formal arrangements to delay payment. The most common form is the institutional mortgage (including Veterans Administration and Federal Housing Administration mortgages given by banks and savings and loans).

If you have taken out an *equity line* against your home or other real estate, you probably have a second or third mortgage against the property. (The *equity line* is a line of credit given by a lender using the equity you have in your real property as collateral.) If the seller loaned you money to buy the property, he or she probably has a *purchase money mortgage.*

A *second mortgage* is a loan for which some additional value in the real property was given as collateral after the original, or primary mortgage. In order to help you buy the property, the seller may have given you a second or even a third mortgage. In many cases these are interest only, or amortized over a long period of time with a balloon payment due in five years or so. Also, if a lender loans you money to make improvements to the property (or for other purposes previously explained in Chapter 7), the lender may have taken out a second or third mortgage on your property.

Any other lender who holds a mortgage on your property, or anyone who has a lien against your property either by virtue of a judgment or otherwise (as explained in Chapter 2) besides the first mortgage holder, can foreclose its mortgage. However, when title to the property is transferred at the foreclosure sale, the buyer will get the property subject to the first or prior mortgages.

The important point to remember is this—if you have several mortgages against your property, keeping the first one current is not enough. If you do not keep the others current, a *foreclosure* action may still be filed by the other mortgage holders, who would then foreclose their interest in your property subject to the first or prior mortgages. They may then pay off the first or prior mortgages.

Example: Bank A has a mortgage on your property. Bank B has a second mortgage. You pay Bank A the regular payments, but not Bank B. Bank B may foreclose, take title to the property subject to the Bank A mortgage.

NOTE: *A mortgage can be foreclosed only through court action.*

CONTRACT OR AGREEMENT FOR DEED

In some states the "Contract for Deed," "Agreement for Deed," or "Land Contract" is still used, where title to the property does not actually transfer to the buyer until a certain specified amount of money is paid toward the purchase. Although your seller may have led you to believe that, if you do not pay, he may immediately reclaim the property and require you to leave, you should confirm that fact with an attorney.

In many states the seller must go through formal foreclosure proceedings just as if title had transferred when the sale was made. The law often provides a purchaser under a Contract or Agreement for Deed with *equitable title* to the property and will protect that interest as it does the interest of an actual legal title holder. To protect your interest as purchaser of the property, you should determine whether the Contract or Agreement for Deed can be recorded in your local public records. This will put others on notice of your interest in the property.

A seller under a Contract for Deed may require you to sign a *quitclaim deed* at the time you signed the Contract for Deed, allowing the seller to record the transfer of title back to him or her if you fail to make the payments as required. You should check the law in your state to determine whether this is legal. In some states such a deed or transfer of title back to the seller at the time you signed the Contract or Agreement for Deed would be *void* (or *voidable*).

125

DEED OF TRUST

Many states use the *deed of trust* as the form of indebtedness to the lender. This involves three parties—the beneficiary or lender, the trustor or borrower, and the trustee, an independent third party that holds the trust deed. The trust deed is the document signed over by you, the borrower, to the trustee, that gives the trustee the power to sell your property if you fail to make the payments required on the note you signed promising to make payments to the lender.

YOUR LOAN DOCUMENTS

Your note and mortgage, trust deed, or other loan documents should spell out the terms of your loan, including the total amount of the mortgage and the monthly payments. You may also have a *grace period*—a specified number of days to make the payment—before late payment charges or additional interest can be added. Review all the documents carefully and, if you do not understand them, call your lender and ask. Most mortgages must meet the Truth in Lending requirements explained in Chapter 7.

THE MORTGAGE FORECLOSURE PROCESS

Although the procedural details may vary from state to state, a mortgage foreclosure generally works like this: Your lender will notify you that your payment is late, and that it must be brought current. If that particular payment and subsequent payments are not made, the lender will notify you that if you do not pay the required amount, the lender will begin foreclosure proceedings. (The lender usually uses an attorney at this point.)

A lawsuit is then filed, advising the court that no payments have been received for the specified time period, that the lender is exercising its right to *accelerate* the mortgage, and that the lender is entitled to foreclose its mortgage. In other words, the lender is asking that the property be taken from you by court order and sold to the highest bidder, and that any interest you have be *foreclosed*.

After the lawsuit is filed, you will be either served with a summons or notice of the foreclosure will be published in the local paper that publishes legal notices. There is a period of time in which responses must be filed. If you do not file any written defenses with the court, which happens often, the case is set for hearing. The judge will then order that the mortgage be foreclosed and that a date for sale be set. Notice of the sale is published, and the property is sold to the highest bidder. (Usually either the sheriff's office or clerk of the court conducts the sale.)

SERVICE OF PROCESS AND DEFICIENCY JUDGMENTS

If the lender or mortgage holder (plaintiff) makes a diligent effort and is still unable to find you in order to have you personally served with the summons from the court, in most cases notice of the foreclosure lawsuit can be published in a local newspaper. If you are served only by publication—in other words, you are not personally served with a summons—then the lender can take the property and no more. However, if you are *properly* served with a summons, and the property does not sell at the foreclosure sale for the amount awarded in the court's judgment of foreclosure, you may be held personally liable for any deficiency. A *deficiency* is the difference between the amount of the judgment and the lesser amount of the actual sale price.

Example: If the judgment was for $100,000 and the property sold for only $90,000, there is a $10,000 deficiency.

Again, this will depend upon the terms of your particular note and mortgage.

A deficiency judgment is like any other judgment and the same options are available to the creditor (the former mortgage holder) for collection. In some states the deficiency judgment is entered automatically; in others, the creditor must go to the court after the sale and ask that judgment be entered.

NOTE: *California does not allow a first mortgage holder to get a deficiency judgment; a few other states restrict the availability of a deficiency judgment.*

You can argue to the court that the lender should not be granted a deficiency judgment against you if the sale price for the property at the foreclosure sale was unreasonably low. The court has the right to look into the relationship between the lender and the buyer of your property and decide whether there was any misconduct or *collusion* (secret agreement between the lender and the buyer), in which case a judge can refuse to enter a deficiency judgment. If the value of the property exceeds the debt, the judge can refuse to give the lender a deficiency judgment against you.

At this stage of the proceeding you need to present as much evidence as possible to the court, including an appraisal of the property's fair market value, which might cause a judge to decide in your favor. If you can afford it, you may want to have an appraisal of the property done on the date of sale.

If the property sells at the foreclosure sale for an amount higher than the amount of the judgment plus any added-on legal interest, then you may be entitled to the excess amount.

AFTER THE SALE—PERIOD OF REDEMPTION

Most states have a *period of redemption* after the sale takes place where the owner can pay the amount of the judgment to the court, plus any legal interest, and redeem his property. This time period is set by law, and varies from state to state. As another possible solution to the foreclosure, you may be able to transfer (or *assign*) this right to redeem your property to someone else, who can then in turn either lease or sell the property back to you.

FORECLOSING A DEED OF TRUST

A trust deed is advantageous to the lender because the lender does not have to go to court to foreclose its loan. If you do not meet your obligations under the note, a notice of default can be recorded in your local county records. *Once it is recorded and you have received a copy, the foreclosure process has begun.* Most states give you a certain period of time, after the notice is recorded and you have received your copy, to reinstate your loan. In order to reinstate the loan, you must bring the payments current and pay any interest and penalties.

After the period allowed for reinstatement has run, the trustee must advertise the property for sale for a minimum period of time. You will find the advertisement in a paper containing legal notices—probably not in your regular newspaper. After the time for advertising has run, the property is sold to the highest bidder. Often the lender (in this case the *beneficiary*) is the highest bidder. Following the sale, your state may give you an additional period of time to redeem the property.

SELLING THE PROPERTY BEFORE FORECLOSURE

If you sell the property before the lender forecloses, your buyer, the title insurance company, or attorney handling the closing will research the title and find that the property has a mortgage or deed of trust (or mortgages or liens) against it. Sometimes a buyer takes title to the property in spite of the mortgage (instead of paying off the mortgage and getting a mortgage release or satisfaction), and assumes and agrees with you that he or she will make the mortgage payments to you or directly to the lender. However, your obligation to make the payments has not automatically been eliminated.

Many mortgages and notes contain a *due on sale clause*. In other words, if there is a transfer of title without the lender's approval, the lender may declare the entire balance of the mortgage due and payable in full. Although beyond the scope of this book, you should carefully review your loan documents before considering such a transfer. Even if there is no due-on-sale clause, you will not be relieved of the debt. Many bank loans require that a new buyer qualify and pay a certain amount to the bank before the bank will relieve you and accept the new owner as the borrower.

If you do not get a release from your lender, the lender can proceed with foreclosure if your buyer does not make the payments as he promised you. Not only will your buyer be named as a defendant in the foreclosure lawsuit, but you will also be named as a defendant as the person obligated on note and mortgage. The lender may still get a deficiency judgment against you.

Example: Beverly bought a home in Florida from John. John gave Beverly a deed to the property, and Beverly in turn gave John a note and mortgage. John financed eighty percent of the purchase price of the property. Beverly then sold the property to Charles, and Charles agreed to make the payments to John. When Charles failed to continue making payments, John filed a lawsuit to foreclose his mortgage on the property. Beverly, although she had sold the property to Charles, was named as a defendant in the lawsuit. John had no agreement with Charles-only with Beverly. The property was purchased at the foreclosure sale for less than the amount of money owed on the mortgage plus attorneys fees and court costs. John asked the court to enter a deficiency judgment against Beverly for the difference.

DEED IN LIEU OF FORECLOSURE

If you find yourself in a position where you are simply unable to continue making your payments and cannot sell your property, you may want to suggest to your lender that it take a *deed in lieu of foreclosure*. This is a deed transferring title of the property to the lender, in exchange for the lender's agreement to forego the foreclosure proceeding and forego obtaining a deficiency judgment against you (in a state that allows deficiency judgments in mortgage foreclosures). In your negotiations, you should also ask that the lender allow you to live in the property for a certain period of time after the transfer of title.

Not all lenders will accept this as an alternative, especially if you have other assets and the lender believes it can collect a deficiency judgment. Most lenders would prefer not to own real estate, particularly where the value of the property is less than the amount of the mortgage. However, this is an alternative that you may wish to consider.

A deed in lieu of foreclosure may be a good alternative if the mortgage holder is the person from whom you bought the property. The seller would then have the property back to sell again, and he will also have had the benefit of the down payment you paid when you bought the property.

NOTE: *Since this is recorded in your local public records, a credit reporting agency may report the deed in lieu of foreclosure on your credit report.*

NEGOTIATING WITH YOUR LENDER

Your lender may also be willing to work with you during *economic hardships,* and take partial payments for a period of time or forego payments until you are able to resume the regular payment schedule. (Particularly in bad economic times, lenders usually do not want to own your real estate—they want the money. Even if they get the property back through foreclosure, they probably will not be able to get the money.) You and the lender are, in most cases, looking for the same thing—a way in which the bank can minimize its losses and you can keep the property. As a result of the large number of delinquencies in home loans, some lenders have even established departments for the specific purpose of working out loan payment problems with borrowers.

When you realize you are having financial difficulties, do the following.

- Set an appointment with the bank's loan department manager, or have a personal meeting with the officer who is in charge of your loan. (You should begin with a positive attitude—that you are willing to work out your financial problem *with* the lender.)

- Explain your circumstances, and that you are committed to meeting your obligations.

- Empathize with the lender's position in a tough financial market.

- If the officer is not responding favorably to your appeal, you should point out that you may consider bankruptcy as an option. This would tie up the property for a considerable length of time, and cost the lender both interest and legal fees. (If you file bankruptcy, the lender probably will not be able to get a deficiency judgment against you.) The officer may well decide it is much better to negotiate with you than to take such a loss.

An individual or private lender may be willing to work with you through your difficult times, particularly if you had previously been prompt in making your payments. In negotiating with a private lender, you should find out what the lender does or intends to do with the loan payment. Perhaps he will extend your loan in exchange for an increase in the interest rate. It is important to consider a number of different alternatives.

FHA Extensions

If you have Federal Housing Administration (FHA) loan on your house, you may be able to work out an extension of your payments. The FHA insures the loans that institutional lenders make to you. If you default on your FHA loan, the lender may turn the property over to FHA and collect its money. In order to help you stay out of foreclosure, the FHA has a plan that may help you.

If you are behind three months or more on your payments, your lender will send you a letter regarding your default and a form for you to complete explaining your financial situation. After receiving your completed form, the lender can then transfer your loan to the Department of Housing and Urban Development

(HUD). Or, you may contact your local HUD office directly and explain that you have an FHA insured mortgage and that you are unable to make the payments due to circumstances beyond your control (usually an illness or job lay-off).

NOTE: *The property must be your primary residence and your only FHA property.*

You must also be able to show that you will be able to begin making payments again within a certain time period. If you meet the requirements, a plan will be worked out where you will have a certain time period to bring the payments current.

More detailed information on this program is available through your local HUD office.

If you have a *balloon payment* (the term usually refers to a payment that is more than twice larger than any other payment under the loan) coming due that you are unable to make, try to get your lender to refinance the loan. You may be able to make larger payments over a period of time and pay off the balance due. With some creative thought and a clear idea of what your lender's objectives are, you may be able to come up with some alternatives to pay the balance due.

All possibilities should be explored before you allow the foreclosure process to go forward, find yourself served with a summons and then possibly have a deficiency judgment entered against you. Remember, both the foreclosure action and the judgment will be shown on your credit report and may negatively affect your ability to get credit in the future.

IF YOU ARE IN THE MILITARY

The Soldiers' and Sailors' Civil Relief Act (the current act dates back to 1940) provides an umbrella of protection from civil legal actions for certain military personnel. (U.S.C., Title 50 "War and National Defense Act.") A lender cannot foreclose out of court (on a deed of trust) if you are in the military service. The plaintiff in a court foreclosure action must file a sworn statement with the court stating whether or not you are in the military service. If the plaintiff states that either (1) he does not know, or (2) you are in the military service, the court cannot enter a judgment against you until an attorney has been appointed to represent you and the attorney is heard on your behalf.

RECAP—STEPS YOU CAN TAKE AFTER FORECLOSURE IS STARTED

Recently the news media has presented numerous stories about foreclosures, particularly in those areas of the country hardest hit economically. Your best approach is to negotiate with your lender *before* the foreclosure process is started and reach an agreement to extend, refinance, or otherwise work out your problem. In some cases, of course, there is not much you can do to prevent the inevitable. Once the foreclosure process has begun, you can still stop or at least delay the process by:

• reaching an agreement with the lender that will reduce your payment for a period of time (*forbearance agreement*). The lender may accept whatever you are able to pay, and accrue the balance owed over time to be added onto the mortgage, or give you an extension, turning the missed payments into a debt payable during or after the original term of the loan;

- if there is a second (or third, etc.) loan against your property, negotiating with that lender to pay off the first loan and incorporate the amount into the second, resulting in only one loan for you to pay;

- reading your loan papers carefully to determine whether you have the right to bring the payments current after foreclosure is filed. (Remember that if the loan is in the form of a trust deed, you should be able to bring the payments current before the notice of sale is published.) If so, you may be able to raise the funds to reinstate the loan—i.e., arrange a loan from a friend, refinance through the same or another lender, take in a co-owner or partner who perhaps will help you bring the loan current in exchange for a portion of the equity in the property, etc. You may even have a family member who is willing to co-sign or give you a loan to help you through your crisis;

- in a mortgage foreclosure, filing your written response to the foreclosure action with the court. The court will then allow both you and the lender to present your cases. In your written response, you should dispute any inaccuracies in your lender's figures, inaccuracies in the legal description, or other lender errors, and present as a *counterclaim* against the foreclosure complaint any claim you have against the lender for violation of the Truth in Lending disclosure requirements (see Chapter 7);

- in a mortgage foreclosure action, telling the court that service was improper. Even after the sale, in some instances you may be able to have the entire foreclosure set aside (made null and void) by the court if you can show that you were available to be served by the lender. Yet, instead of personally serving you with a summons, notice was published in the newspaper;

- challenging the trust deed documents in court. By proving to the court that the documents do not include information required by law, the entire foreclosure process can be made null and void. Regulation Z requirements must be met in most situations (see Chapter 7);

- getting your lender to agree to accept a deed in lieu of foreclosure, if you have no defense and you can avoid a deficiency judgment; or

- using the threat of (or filing) bankruptcy.

You may have a lawsuit against the lender if they have threatened you or attempted to intimidate you. You should set these facts out in your written defense to the foreclosure. The Federal Trade Commission has the authority to protect you from a lender's unfair and deceptive practices used in foreclosure.

On pages 141-143 is a mortgage foreclosure complaint and a sample response (*answer*). In your response to a court action, you should first answer each statement made by the lender in the complaint. Then, if you agree that some of the statements made by the lender in the complaint are correct, but you have further explanations or reasons that you believe the court should be made aware of, these should be set out in your answer as *affirmative defenses*. If you have any claim against the lender—for example, violation of a disclosure requirement under Regulation Z—this should be stated in a counterclaim or countersuit along with your answer to the lender's charges.

It is possible to have a foreclosure judgment set aside (withdrawn) even after the redemption period has passed, if you can show to the court that the lender did not make a sufficient effort to find and notify you, or that some other error occurred in the foreclosure action.

Finally, borrowers are fighting back against lenders who were once aggressively competing for the borrowers' business. Lawsuits range from a 1.5 billion dollar claim based on fraud and conspiracy in forcing a silver and oil business into bankruptcy, to damages caused by a lender's delays in processing loans. If you think you may have the basis for a lawsuit against your lender, you should get the advice of an attorney.

FOR FURTHER RESEARCH

To determine whether your state uses deeds of trust or mortgages, simply look at your loan documents. Then obtain information from your lender regarding Regulation Z and contact your regional Federal Trade Commission office for further literature (See Appendix C). If your mortgage might be foreclosed, read your state's statutes regarding the legal procedure for filing a foreclosure action, noting the maximum time periods allowed for the various steps in the process.

Note how long you have to redeem your property after the sale. When you research your state's statutes, ask the librarian for an *annotated* version. This will include cases that might help clarify certain provisions of the law. The cases will also give you an idea of what kinds of defenses other people in situations similar to yours have presented to the court.

Your local law library might have how-to books on mortgage foreclosure defenses such as those published by your state bar association continuing legal education committee. HUD publishes information about how to avoid foreclosure, available via the website at:

http://www.hud.gov/foreclosure/index.cfm

The applicable provision of the Soldiers' and Sailors' Civil Relief Act is found in the United States Code, Appendix 50, Section 532.

RESPONDING TO A FORECLOSURE COMPLAINT

A complaint for foreclosure will usually contain numbered paragraphs, stating why the mortgage is entitled to foreclose. You will need to respond to each statement in the complaint, by either admitting or denying them.

The sample answer on page 142 is based on a complaint that contains the following numbered paragraphs alleging that:

SAMPLE MORTGAGE FORECLOSURE COMPLAINT

IN THE CIRCUIT COURT OF THE NINTH JUDICIAL CIRCUIT IN AND
FOR LEE COUNTY, FLORIDA

<u>XYZ Mortgage Corp.</u>)		
Plaintiff,)		
)		
vs.)	Case No. <u>97-0734</u>	
)		
<u>John Doe and Jane Doe</u>)		
Defendants.)		

<u>FORECLOSURE COMPLAINT</u>

The plaintiff, XYZ Bank, hereby files this complaint as follows:

1. This is an action to foreclose a mortgage on real property located in Lee County, Florida, and for damages in excess of $5,000.00.

2. On or about June 9, 2000, the defendants executed and delivered a note to the plaintiff secured by a mortgage on the real property that is the subject of this action. Copies of the note and mortgage are attached hereto as Exhibits "A" and "B," respectively, and the terms thereof are incorporated herein by reference. The real property that is the subject of this action is described in the mortgage.

3. The defendants failed to pay the installment under the note due, despite demand therefor by the plaintiff.

4. There is now due and owing under the note the principal sum of $39,278.24, together with accrued interest to March 1, 2001 in the amount of $262.50, plus per diem thereafter at the rate of $8.63.

5. The lien represented by the mortgage is superior to the estate or interest of the defendants and anyone claiming by, through or under the defendants.

6. That the property which is the subject of this action is residential rental property, and that a receiver should be appointed by the court to insure the continued maintenance and care of the subject property.

7. The plaintiff has retained the services of the undersigned law firm and has agreed to pay said firm a reasonable fee for the prosecution of this action.

8. All conditions precedent to the institution of this action have occurred, been performed or excused.

WHEREFORE, plaintiff prays that judgment be entered in its favor, and for all other relief the Court deems proper.

Signed	Date

SAMPLE ANSWER TO FORECLOSURE COMPLAINT

IN THE CIRCUIT COURT OF THE NINTH JUDICIAL CIR-
CUIT IN AND FOR LEE COUNTY, FLORIDA

XYZ Mortgage Corp.   )
       Plaintiff,   )
)
vs.   )   Case No. 97-0734
)
John Doe and Jane Doe)
       Defendants.   )

ANSWER

COME NOW the Defendants, ___John Doe and Jane Doe___
_____, and for their answer to
Plaintiff's Complaint, state as follows:

1. Paragraphs 1 and 2 are admitted.
2. Paragraphs 3 and 4 are denied.
3. Defendants are without knowledge to either admit or deny paragraph 5.
4. Paragraph 6 is denied.
5. Defendants are without knowledge to either admit or deny paragraph 7.
6. Paragraph 8 is denied.

WHEREFORE, defendants respectfully request that the court grant judgment in their favor, and for such other and further relief as the court deems proper.

AFFIRMATIVE DEFENSES

11. The amount currently due under the Note and Mortgage is $72,695.98, not the amount the plaintiff claims is due.

12. Defendants offered plaintiff the amount due on July 23, 2001, but plaintiff refused to accept payment.

WHEREFORE, defendants respectfully request that judgment be granted in their favor, and for such other relief as the Court deems proper.

COUNTERCLAIM

1. Plaintiff failed to provide defendants with the correct financial disclosures as required under the Federal Truth in Lending Act, specifically set forth as follows: Plaintiff failed to properly calculate and inform Defendants of the annual percentage rate of interest.

2. As a result of such failure to provide defendants with the correct financial disclosures, defendants have suffered damages in the amount of approximately $10,000 as follows: Excess interest paid in the amount of $7,248.73, plus additional damages to be proven at trial.

3. Plaintiff has threatened defendants for nonpayment by threatening to contact defendants' employers and neighbors.

WHEREFORE, defendants pray that judgment be granted in their favor in the amount of $10,000.00, and for such other relief as the Court deems proper.

Dated: September 12, 2001.

_____

_____

John Doe & Jane Doe, Defendants

12 Easy St., Ft. Myers, FL 99999

Tel. (813) 555-5555

Other sample affirmative defenses which may be inserted in the Answer (paragraph 12):

1. "defendant was not properly served with summons."

2. "the property described in plaintiff's complaint is not the property which is described in plaintiff's loan documents."

3. "defendant has been properly maintaining the property."

A copy of this Answer should be sent to the plaintiff and anyone else required by the court.

Note: *Some states require that you explain very specifically in your complaint or answer the facts surrounding your claim; others allow you to be more general and leave the specifics to be spelled out a later date during the court proceedings.*

REPOSSESSION OF PERSONAL PROPERTY— FORECLOSURE

11

When you buy a car and get financing, you normally give the lender or bank a security interest (lien) in the vehicle. Your state might not require any additional notice of the security interest in property to which you hold a title other than the notice that is placed by the lender directly on the title. On other personal property without a title, the bank or financing company may file what is known as a *financing statement*, which serves the same purpose as a mortgage or deed of trust on real estate. The statement is recorded in the appropriate state office (usually the secretary of state or your county).

It is the lender's duty to make sure that its security interest is properly filed. The financing statement must contain the lender's and your signatures, must clearly identify the property, and must be filed in the correct place.

Just as in a sale of real estate, when you sell the property, the lien must be satisfied or the buyer takes the property with lien still against it (meaning the buyer does not get it without a claim, or "lien-free") and you will still be responsible for payment. The lender can, of course, consent to the transfer of the property and release you from your responsibility. (You may also be violating a provision of your loan agreement and subjecting yourself to criminal and civil prosecution by selling the property without paying off the lender.)

Unless you have an agreement with the lender to the contrary, if you do not pay, or if you otherwise do not live up to your agreement with the lender (such as failing to maintain the required insurance or letting the property deteriorate), the lender has the right to *repossess* the property as long as there is no *breach of the peace* (violation of public peace by riot, disturbance, or otherwise) for example, violation of a curfew or noise ordinance. The lender may then sell it and get a deficiency judgment against you much like the mortgage foreclosure process.

Example: If you have repeatedly missed car loan payments at the bank, the bank may contract with someone to repossess the car. Your car can be picked up wherever it can be found. It is then sold, and you may be held responsible for the difference between the amount it sold for and the amount left on the loan, plus attorneys fees and court costs (the deficiency).

Whoever repossesses the property must do so without breach of the peace. In other words, if the property (furniture or appliances, for example) is located in your home, you must consent to the creditor's entry and repossession. Damage to the property by the creditor while it is being repossessed may be considered a breach of the peace.

However, if the property is accessible without entering your home or a closed building, then there is no breach of the peace.

Example: If your car is parked in your driveway, the creditor may walk up, get into the car and drive it off without violating any law (provided he does not damage the vehicle). If there is damage to your property, you may have a legal case against the lender.

RESTRICTIONS ON REPOSSESSION

The laws regarding secured transactions restrict what the lender can do when repossessing collateral.

• A lender may *not* exert undue pressure on you to repossess an item and has no right to use force.

• A lender is liable to you for any damage caused to the property when it is repossessed.

• A lender may repossess the property without court action only if it can be done without breaching the peace.

SALE OF COLLATERAL AFTER REPOSSESSION

After repossessing the property, the lender may sell it, lease it, or otherwise dispose of it in a commercially reasonable manner. *Commercially reasonable* generally means that the property must be sold in keeping with the prevailing trade and business practices. The property may be sold in its condition at the time of repossession or after reasonable preparation for sale by the creditor.

The proceeds of the sale are applied first to the cost of repossession and selling the property, including attorney's fees and legal expenses if provided for in your agreement. Second, the proceeds go to satisfy the outstanding debt. Third, the proceeds satisfy any other *junior security interest* in the property if the secured party has given proper notice to your creditor.

Requirements for Sale

In order for a creditor to sell collateral, the following requirements must be met:

- The creditor should give you reasonable notice of a sale unless you have waived notice.

- The creditor can purchase your property at a private sale only if the property is sold in a recognized market with standard price quotations *and* if the sale is commercially reasonable. In determining whether a sale is commercially reasonable, the method of sale, time and place of sale, adequacy of advertising, and appropriateness of wholesale versus retail disposition should be considered.

- The creditor must not allow your property to deteriorate after repossession. To do so may be a violation of the creditor's obligations and will adversely affect the creditor's ability to get a deficiency judgment against you.

Depending upon the terms of your security agreement, you may be liable for any *deficiency*—the difference between the amount of the sale applied to satisfy the debt and the total amount due the creditor. Just as in a mortgage foreclosure, you can argue against the deficiency judgment if you are able to show to the court that the lender sold the property for far too little money.

The lender should also notify you of the sale of the property in order to get a deficiency judgment.

Example: If you loan your car to a friend, the car is wrecked and the lender accepts the insurance proceeds and turns the car over to the insurance company without notifying you, the lender cannot get a deficiency judgment against you for the balance owed.

If you have paid at least sixty percent of the cash price of the property, after repossession the creditor must sell the property within ninety days or you may have a lawsuit against the creditor for *conversion* (taking your property and converting it to the creditor's own use), or as set forth in the section "Your Remedies" in this chapter.

LENDER'S PATTERN OF ACCEPTING LATE PAYMENTS

If your lender has consistently accepted late payments from you, you may have a defense. The lender's conduct led you to believe that late payments would be accepted and that you would be allowed to catch up. The lender's conduct indicated that you should have been given notice of a change in the lender's policy.

YOUR REMEDIES

You have several remedies if your lender is attempting to take your property for payment of a debt, including defending the lawsuit or paying to take back the property. Following are some of the options available.

Soldiers' and Sailors' Civil Relief Act

The Soldiers' and Sailors' Civil Relief Act of 1940 provides protections from civil lawsuits or actions for certain military personnel. (See page 136 for more details.) If you entered into the agreement to buy personal property, such as a refrigerator or automobile, before you entered the military, the creditor cannot repossess the property without a court order. Before allowing the property to be repossessed, the court has the option to decide what is in the best interest of both parties. For example, you might be allowed to keep the property in return for smaller payment amounts to creditor.

No Proper Financing Statement

When the lender attempts to take the collateral, you may argue that the financing statement was not properly filed, or that it failed to contain certain vital information, and that therefor the lender does not have valid security interest in the property.

Your Right to Redeem the Property

Any time before the creditor has sold the property, or before your debt has been paid, you may *redeem* (take back) the property by paying to the creditor all obligations that the property secured plus any expenses the creditor incurred in taking it and preparing for its sale, including reasonable attorney fees and costs.

Reimbursement for Loss

You may recover from the creditor any loss the creditors caused by failing to comply with the requirements regarding repossession and sale of the property. If the property is consumer goods, then you have a right to recover at least the amount of the credit service charge plus ten percent of the principle amount of the debt.

Example: If the creditor repossessed your boat and allowed the physical condition and value to drastically decline while keeping it for many months, failed to follow its normal repossession procedures, continued to hold it even after it filed its lawsuit for foreclosure, then sold the boat at a price less than half of its value when repossessed, you have a claim against the creditor in that the sale was not "commercially reasonable." (*First Florida National Bank at Pensacola v. Martin*, App. 1 Dist., 449 So. 2d 861 (1984).)

Punitive Damages

Finally, you may be entitled to punitive damages if you can show that the creditor grossly disregarded your rights.

Example: Where a seller had repossessed the buyer's car without warning, seller's agent inventoried the personal property in the car and yet returned the personal property to the car contrary to normal creditor procedure, the court agreed that the seller had shown wanton disregard for the buyer's rights to his personal property and gave the buyer an award of punitive damages against the seller in the amount of $1,000. (*Ford Motor Credit Co. v. Waters*, App. 273 So.2d 96, (1973).)

IF THE LENDER ALREADY HAS THE COLLATERAL

Your lender may have a security interest in your property simply by taking possession of it.

Example: If you have given your bank stocks and bonds to hold as collateral for a note you've signed, the bank may have the right to immediately sell the stocks and bonds if you do not make the required payments. The bank will apply the proceeds from the sale to the unpaid debt, plus any costs of the sale. Unless you have made other arrangements with the lender, the balance, if any is left, should be given back to you.

The same requirements for a commercially reasonable sale of repossessed property apply to a sale of property the lender already has in its possession.

FOR FURTHER RESEARCH

Your state statutes should include a section on *secured transactions*, in which you will find the rights and duties of the lender and borrower set forth in detail.

In addition, your state's consumer affairs office should have information available regarding your rights.

The applicable provision of the Soldiers' and Sailors' Civil Relief Act is found in the appendix of the United States Code, 50, Ap. 531.

WHEN THE CREDITOR FILES A LAWSUIT 12

If you have not been able to reach an agreement with your creditors as to how and when payment will be made, there is a good possibility that you will be sued. The goal of the creditor is to get you to pay the debt, or to take your property and sell it in order to pay the debt. Unless the lawsuit is dismissed or withdrawn from the court, a judgment will be entered, either for or against you. (You may be able to work out a "deferred" judgment with the creditor, where the lawsuit is dismissed once payments are made. This will be discussed in more detail below.)

JUDGMENT

A *judgment* is a decision made by a court in a lawsuit. It becomes part of the public records that are available to anyone who takes the time to obtain the information, including credit reporting agencies. A money judgment requires you to pay a certain dollar amount.

HOW A CREDITOR GETS A JUDGMENT

A money judgment is obtained by first filing a lawsuit in the appropriate court. A *lawsuit* is an action where the *plaintiff*, the person who files the lawsuit, asks the court to make a determination that he or she is entitled to money from you. The *petition* or *complaint* is the document that the plaintiff files with the court, stating what he feels he is entitled to and why. In legal terminology, the plaintiff is asking the court for *relief*. (Deficiency judgments are discussed in Chapters 10 and 11.) The *defendant* is the person the lawsuit is filed against and who the plaintiff claims owes the money.

The procedures for filing a lawsuit and getting a judgment vary somewhat from one state to another, and are governed by your state court's Rules of Civil Procedure. These rules are available in your state's *statute* books, which you should be able to find at your nearest law library, or perhaps your local public library. Your local court clerk may also be able to answer specific questions such as how a document must be filed or the time deadline for filing.

Your creditor may file a lawsuit against you if you do not pay the monies you owe. Depending upon the dollar amount the creditor is suing for and your state's laws regulating the court system, the creditor may file on his own in *small claims court*, or a court in which an individual can file without an attorney up to a maximum dollar amount. This is usually the least expensive method of filing a lawsuit that can be used by the creditor.

Attorney's Fees

If you have a written contract with your creditor, or if your state laws so provide, the creditor may be entitled to attorney's fees if he wins the lawsuit and the court enters a judgment against you. If this is the case, the creditor will often choose to use an attorney rather than file the lawsuit himself, even if the dollar amount is small.

Most bank loan documents require that you pay the attorneys fees and costs of any action taken against you to collect the money. You should read the documents carefully to determine whether the attorneys fees are chargeable against you even if the lender is unsuccessful.

If your state has a law that allows attorneys fees to be charged to you only if there is *no justiciable issue*, (in other words, there is absolutely no question about your liability for the amount due), then you should by all means raise a defense.

Summons

Once the lawsuit is filed, you must be served with a summons issued by the court, along with a copy of the petition or complaint. *If you are not served with summons and a copy of the - petition or complaint, a judgment for payment of money usually cannot be entered against you in the court records.* The summons and petition or complaint will in most cases be served by either a sheriff's deputy or by a special process server appointed by the court.

Answer

You will have a certain period of time to answer the lawsuit after you are served, or a date and time to appear in court will be on the summons. If you are unable to determine your deadline from the papers, call the court clerk in the courthouse where the lawsuit was filed—the clerk should be able to tell you when your answer is due.

If you choose to answer the lawsuit yourself, you should make sure that you respond to each one of the charges set forth in the petition or complaint. Sample complaints and answers are included on pages 164-165. If you let your deadline go by without responding or appearing as required, a *default judgment* may be entered against you. In other words, the court may grant the creditor's request and enter the judgment requiring you to pay.

Interest

After the judgment is granted by the court, it may continue to accrue interest until the date it is paid. The amount of interest varies from state to state.

YOUR DEFENSES TO THE PETITION OR COMPLAINT

If you do not care whether a default judgment is entered against you, and you do not have a defense to any of the charges in the creditor's complaint, then you do not need to do anything. Before you decide to do nothing, however, you should consider the defenses you may have to your creditor's demand for payment. Possible defenses are:

- the creditor has already been paid;

- the service for which the creditor is claiming payment was not performed;

- you are not responsible for payment of the debt (i.e., the debt was incurred by a corporation—not you personally, or by your spouse—not you);

- you were not properly served with summons;

- the *statute of limitations* has lapsed—in other words, the time allowed the creditor to file suit against you for collection of the debt has passed. (The statutes of limitations in each state are found at the end of this book in Appendix D.)

- the creditor's actions in getting your promise to pay were *unconscionable*, or in other words, so outrageous and overbearing that they would shock the average person. You are telling the court that you were so taken advantage of that you had practically no alternative but to agree to the creditor's terms.

NOTE: *In order for this defense to be effective, you should have notified the creditor immediately after you agreed to pay that you wanted to cancel your agreement and the reasons why. Your defense would be even stronger if you also refused to make any payments to the creditor and, if the creditor provided you with a service such as roof repair, you immediately requested that he discontinue the work;*

- the goods you received were defective and therefore you do not owe the money;

- the creditor has breached its warranty, (i.e., has not met the conditions it is required to meet under the warranty(ies) you received with the goods you purchased.) In addition to any written warranties you received when you purchased the goods, there may be *implied warranties* (i.e., warranties that the creditor or seller gives you just by selling you the product). For example, the goods must be fit for the purpose for which they are intended to be used;

- if a creditor is suing you for a deficiency judgment after repossessing and selling collateral, you may defend on the basis that the sale was not in a *commercially reasonable manner*. (See Chapter 10.); and

- specifically for child support, you have lost your job and request a reduction. (See page 163 for a sample motion of this nature.)

If you were not properly served, the case should not proceed in court. Once you become aware that a judgment has been entered against you based on improper service of summons, you should immediately notify the court clerk and ask about the procedure to have the judgment set-aside (i.e., withdrawn from the court records). This may require you to appear in court and present your argument to the judge.

After the lawsuit has been properly filed and summons properly served, there are legally prescribed methods by which the attorney or plaintiff may obtain information from you and other persons regarding the claim. Ultimately, if you do not have any legitimate defenses against the lawsuit and you have been unable to settle with your creditor, the court may enter a judgment against you.

After the judgment is granted by the court, there may also be a certain period of time that you have to appeal the judgment or ask the court to rehear your case and modify or set aside the judgment before the judgment creditor can begin efforts to collect on the judgment. If you have defenses that you did not bring up at the trial or before the judgment was entered, now is the time to let the court know. You may also have the right to appeal your case to a higher court.

MOVING TO ANOTHER STATE

A creditor can take its judgment into the state where you are currently living or where your assets are located. There is a legal procedure where the original judgment can become a new judgment in another state. (Check to see if your state has adopted the Uniform Enforcement of Foreign Judgments Act.) The new state laws regarding collection of the judgment will then apply to the judgment creditor. You should be notified either by service of a summons or by certified mail from the court clerk that the judgment is being filed, and be given an opportunity to contest the judgment before any action is taken to collect it.

CONFESSION OF JUDGMENT

A *confession of judgment* provision in a loan document gives the creditor the right to automatically get a judgment against you if you do not pay the balance owed. Such a provision is prohibited by federal law except in a real estate contract. If your loan document contains such a provision, it is not enforceable by the creditor.

POSSIBLE ALTERNATIVES IF THE DEBT IS LEGITIMATE

There are several options available to you if the money is legitimately owed and you have no defenses to a lawsuit. Among the options are the following.

Reduced Lump-Sum Settlement

If the debt for which the creditor is demanding payment is legitimate and you have determined that you have no defenses, perhaps your creditor would be willing to settle the debt with you before he obtains a judgment. (As will be discussed in following chapters, *executing* on a judgment is often more difficult than getting the judgment.)

It may be more appealing to your creditor to receive a lump sum reduced amount as payment in full, rather than go to the time and expense of obtaining a judgment and then attempting to collect the amount due under the judgment.

Deferred Judgment

If the creditor has already filed his lawsuit, and if you are unable to pay a lump sum amount as settlement in exchange for having the lawsuit dismissed, you might suggest to the creditor that he take a *deferred* judgment. If you pay an agreed-upon amount until the balance due is paid in full, the lawsuit should then be dismissed without a judgment ever being entered against you. However, if you fail to make the required payments, the plaintiff creditor need only properly notify the court, and the court may sign the judgment.

Mediation and Arbitration

As an alternative to court, you can suggest to the creditor that you take your dispute to an independent, third party who will hear both sides. This can be either an arbitrator or a mediator. An *arbitrator* will hear both sides and then make a decision for you just like a court would do. A *mediator* will talk to both sides and attempt to help them come to a mutually acceptable agreement. Some states have mediation programs available to parties in dispute.

Going to Court

If your creditor is unwilling to either settle and dismiss the lawsuit or take a deferred judgment, prepare to go to court. If you are not represented by an attorney, you should have your income and assets well-documented, as well as your monthly expenses and your repayment plan. (See Chapter 13.)

When the creditor recognizes that you are making the best effort possible to repay the debt, it is likely that settlement will be reached before the case is actually heard by the judge. In most cases, this will be less costly for the creditor than monthly garnishments or other methods of collecting the judgment amount. If the case is heard by a judge, the judge may order that the creditor accept the amount of money you have offered to pay.

EFFECT OF JUDGMENT ON CREDIT REPORT

As explained in Chapter 5, "Items Your Report Cannot Contain", page 60, a judgment may remain on your credit record for a period of seven years, unless the law of the state in which the judgment is entered allows a longer time period. State law may also allow the creditor to periodically renew the judgment, so that it remains effective for a much longer period.

With regard to your credit report, you have the options set forth in Chapter 5. Of course you should offer an explanation about the circumstances surrounding the judgment to any potential lender who will review the report in making its decision whether or not to loan you money.

FOR FURTHER RESEARCH

Read your state's statutes regarding the legal procedure for filing a lawsuit, noting the maximum time periods allowed for the various steps in the process. When you research your state's statutes, ask the librarian for an *annotated* version. This will include cases that might help clarify certain provisions of the law. The cases will also give you an idea of what kinds of defenses other people in situations similar to yours have presented to the court. (Your court clerk may also have information about mediation or arbitration services.)

The prohibition against a *confession of judgment* clause is found in Code of Federal Regulations, Title 16, "Commercial Practices" Chapter 1, Part 444 the section of the Federal Trade Commission regulations regarding credit practices.

SAMPLE MOTION FOR MODIFICATION

IN THE CIRCUIT COURT OF THE _____JUDICIAL
CIRCUIT IN AND FOR _____COUNTY, FLORIDA _____

IN RE:)
)
MARY SMITH   )   Case No._____
a minor   )

MOTION FOR MODIFICATION OF CHILD SUPPORT

JOHN SMITH, father of MARY SMITH, hereby requests
that the court reduce the amount of child support
required to be paid under Order dated May 6, 1999,
for the following reasons:
1. I was laid-off from my job at XYZ Company on
March 15, 1999.
2. Although I have made a diligent effort, I have
been unable to find employment at a salary compa-
rable to what I was making at XYZ Company.
3. I am currently working as a gardener for ABC
Landscaping, and my salary is $6.00 per hour, which
is approximately one-half of what I was paid while
employed with XYZ Company.
WHEREFORE, I hereby ask the court that my child
support obligation be reduced to $30.00 per week .

_____
JOHN SMITH

STATE OF FLORIDA)
COUNTY OF HILLSBOROUGH)
       On this_____day of March, 2001, before me, the under-
signed, a Notary Public in and for the above county and State,
appeared JOHN SMITH, who is personally known to me to be the
same person who executed the above Motion, and that he did so
as his free act and deed.

_____
Notary Public

My Commission Expires:

SAMPLE COMPLAINT

IN THE CIRCUIT COURT OF THE SIXTH JUDICIAL CIRCUIT, IN AND FOR PINELLAS COUNTY, FLORIDA

EASY-AIR, INC.,)	
Plaintiff)	
)	
vs.)	Case No. 01-3592
)	
JOE DOE)	
Defendant	

COMPLAINT

Plaintiff, Easy-Air, Inc.,a Florida corporation, states as follows:

1. Defendant Joe Doe resides at 1412 Heatstroke Lane, Clearwater, Florida 34616.

2. Defendant Joe Doe entered into an agreement with Easy-Air, Inc. on May 2, 1999, whereby Plaintiff agreed to sell to Joe Doe a new air conditioning system, to install it and provide any necessary service, for a total price of $2,500;

3. Plaintiff Easy-Air, Inc. delivered and installed the air conditioning system, but Joe Doe has refused to pay;

4. Plaintiff has performed all of its obligations under the agreement with Joe Doe;

5. Joe Doe is obligated to pay Plaintiff Easy-Air, Inc. for the air conditioning system and installation.

WHEREFORE, Plaintiff demands judgment against the Defendant, and for Plaintiff's costs and attorney fees.

Easy-Air, Inc.

By:_____

Its president

164

SAMPLE ANSWER TO COMPLAINT

IN THE CIRCUIT COURT OF THE SIXTH JUDICIAL CIR-
CUIT, IN AND FOR PINELLAS COUNTY, FLORIDA

EASY-AIR, INC._____)
      Plaintiff,)
vs.   )   Case No. 01-3592_
JOE DOE_____)
      Defendant.)

ANSWER

Defendant, Joe Doe, answers plaintiff's Complaint as follows:

1. Defendant admits paragraph 1 of the Complaint.

2. Defendant admits that he entered into a business transaction with plaintiff on May 2, 1999, but denies that he agreed to pay plaintiff.

3. Defendant admits to receiving statements and a demand letter from plaintiff, and defendant responded by sending letters to plaintiff, copies of which are attached to this Answer.

4. Defendant denies paragraphs 4 and 5.

AFFIRMATIVE DEFENSES

1. In exchange for the $2,500.00 defendant was to pay to plaintiff, plaintiff was to deliver to defendant a new air conditioning system, fully installed in the defendant's home.

2. Plaintiff has failed to deliver this item to defendant, therefore, defendant does not owe any money to plaintiff.

WHEREFORE, defendant demands judgment against plaintiff.

           Joe Doe, Defendant
           1412 Heatstroke Ln.
           Clearwater, FL 34616
           (813) 555-5555

COLLECTION OF MONEY JUDGMENTS

13

ACTIONS BY A JUDGMENT CREDITOR

After a creditor gets a judgment against you, he becomes a *judgment creditor*. Once the court enters its judgment, the judgment creditor, if he knows or believes you have or are expecting to receive assets, may attempt to collect the amount due in the judgment in a number of different ways (*execute on the judgment*). The judgment creditor must first determine your assets.

Judgment Creditor's Investigation

If the creditor is unsure of your income and assets, he may obtain this information by taking your *deposition* or asking you to answer *interrogatories* (written questions). Other forms of investigation include checking whether you have a vehicle registered in your name and checking with the property appraiser to find out what, if any, real property you own. If you gave your judgment creditor a financial statement when you obtained the loan, the creditor will also review the statement again to see what assets you represented to him that you own.

In a deposition (or by written interrogatories), the creditor may ask you questions such as the following.

- Are you engaged in your own business and, if so, is the business a sole proprietorship, partnership, or corporation?

- Are you employed; who is your present employer, how much do you earn; and when are your wages paid?

- Do you receive any interest in your employer's business as part of your compensation?

- Do you receive any income from a trust fund?

- Do you receive royalties from any patent, copyright, or invention?

- Do you receive any support from anyone else? If so, from whom and how much?

- Give the names and addresses of all banks in which you have accounts.

- Identify all certificates of deposit, money market accounts, or other accounts where you have money.

- Are you holding any real estate mortgages or other notes (does anyone owe you money)?

- Do you have an interest in a time-share, condominium, or cooperative apartment?

- List your household furnishings, the present value, and whether money is owed against them.

- Do you have any valuable collections, (i.e. stamp, coin, antiques, or other)?

- Do you own any jewelry and, if so, what is the value?

- Do you own any automobile(s), boats, airplanes, motor home, etc.?

- Are you a stockholder in a corporation? If so,what is the name of the corporation and the number of shares of stock you own?

- Do you own any bonds or other securities? If so, give a description.

- Do you have an IRA, Keogh, pension, or any other retirement funds?

- Do you have a life insurance policy with a cash surrender value?

- Are you the beneficiary of a life insurance policy?

- Are you the beneficiary under a will of someone who has died, or do you otherwise expect to inherit money or property?

- Is any money held in trust for you?

- Are you expecting a refund on state or federal income taxes paid?

The creditor may also ask to see your latest tax returns and any other records regarding your income and expenses. The purpose is to determine what property you own that the judgment creditor can attach or take to satisfy the judgment. You must respond to the creditor's request or you may be held in contempt of court. Be careful to answer truthfully, as the penalties for perjury may be far greater than the cost of paying your judgment creditor.

WHEN THE CREDITOR KNOWS WHAT ASSETS YOU HAVE

Once the creditor has obtained information about your assets, he has several options.

Example: A judgment creditor may proceed by garnishing your wages, by seizing an asset such as a car or boat (provided another creditor does not have a prior or *superior claim* to the asset) and selling it, or seizing a bank account.

Some (or all) of your property may be exempt from judgment creditors and the creditor may, by law, be prohibited from taking it. These exemptions are explained in greater detail in Chapter 16. You must be given notice when a judgment creditor is attempting to take your property. The notice should explain how you can file a claim for exemption of the property. The judgment creditor will then either withdraw the attachment or ask for a court hearing.

You are entitled to a hearing to explain to the court that the property is exempt or that it is a basic necessity for you.

Example: If you have a vehicle specially equipped for you due to medical reasons, you will want to explain to the court that the vehicle is absolutely necessary for you to carry out your day-to-day activities, such as grocery shopping.

If you lose the first hearing and your situation changes for the worse, you can ask for a second hearing to explain the change in circumstances to the court and the reasons why the attachment should be withdrawn.

GARNISHMENTS

Garnishment is a procedure used by judgment creditors that results in loss of control over your disposable earnings. Under the Consumer Credit Act garnishment is defined as "any legal or equitable procedure through which the earnings of any individual are required to be withheld for payment of any debt." However, a creditor can also garnish other property such as bank accounts. Wage garnishments are the most common.

Wage Garnishments

Congress has enacted laws, contained in the Consumer Credit Act, Sections 1671 through 1677, that restrict the amount of money a creditor can take through garnishment. These laws apply strictly to wages. Congress reasoned that, if garnishment were freely allowed, creditors would unscrupulously encourage the extension of credit, and repayments would take an excessive portion of one's income, creating economic havoc. Garnishments also often result in loss of employment, which has a negative effect on the national economy.

The intent of the law was to grant exemption to wage earners from burdensome garnishments, to protect employment of wage earners, and to prevent bankruptcies. Your state may have its own exemptions. If your state's garnishment laws are even more restrictive, resulting in smaller garnishments, then the state's laws will take priority over the federal laws; if the state's laws are less restrictive, then the federal laws will apply.

After a judgment is rendered against you by a court of law, your creditor may attempt to garnish your wages. The method of garnishment varies somewhat from state to state, but it is generally available to most creditors to collect money owed them. (Some states allow garnishments before a judgment is actually entered by the court; however, the procedure must be strictly followed by the creditor as with pre-judgment attachments.)

The Garnishment Procedure—Generally

A notice to withhold a certain amount from your wages is first sent to your employer (see the Writ of Garnishment form on page 180). In legal terminology the creditor may now be called the *garnishor.* The employer may now be referred to as the *garnishee.* The garnishee has a certain period of time to respond to the notice ordering the garnishee to pay over to the garnishor certain funds that would otherwise belong to you.

Example: The garnishee may respond by stating that, to the best of his knowledge, you are the head of a household and that therefore your wages are exempt from creditors.

Once the response is received by the garnishor, the garnishor will then decide whether the garnishment should be pursued. This may require a court order. If the garnishment remains intact, then the garnishee must turn the property over to the garnishor. This method of collecting on a judgment is often used as a last resort by creditors, as it is time-consuming and can be expensive.

Federal Exemptions from Wage Garnishment

In some states the wages of a head of a household cannot be garnished at all; in others only a small percentage of the net pay can be garnished. Under federal law, which applies if it is more restrictive than your state's garnishment law, the restrictions on garnishment are as follows:

> The aggregate disposable earnings (compensation for services) which are subject to garnishment cannot exceed twenty-five percent of the wage earner's disposable earnings for that week, or cannot exceed the amount by which the wage earner's disposable earnings for that week exceed thirty times the Federal minimum hourly wage, whichever is less. If the earnings are paid other than on a weekly basis, a multiple of the Federal minimum hourly wage equivalent is prescribed by the Secretary of Labor. (Code of Federal Regulation Title 29, Chapter V, Part 870.10.)

The restrictions do not apply in the case of a court order for support, a filing under Chapter 13 of the Bankruptcy Law, or any debt due for federal or state taxes (see Chapter 14). If you are supporting a spouse or dependent children, the maximum amount of disposable earnings subject to garnishment to enforce a support order (for another spouse or children) is fifty percent. If you are not then currently supporting a spouse or dependent children, then sixty percent of the disposable earnings are subject to garnishment to enforce a support order.

If a support garnishment (garnishment of wages to enforce judgment ordering support) has priority and results in the withholding of twenty-five percent or more of your disposable earnings, another creditor garnishment may not be permitted.

Depending upon your state's laws, filing of a new garnishment action may be required each time the garnishor wishes to collect money. If so, satisfaction of the creditor's judgment becomes a long and tedious process.

The restrictions apply only to wage garnishments, and not to assignments. If you have assigned a portion of your wages to a creditor, the assignment is not subject to the percentage limitations. If you are potentially subject to having your wages or property garnished, you should make it a point to find out exactly how much of your wages can be garnished and at what time intervals. See Chapter 16, pages 202-213 for state by state wage exemptions.

Restrictions on Discharge from Employment as a Result of Garnishment

To protect against hardships and disruptions resulting from garnishment of wages, the federal law has also placed restrictions upon employers. Under the federal law, no employer may discharge any employee for the reason that the employee's earnings have been subject to garnishment for any one indebtedness. However, this does not protect you if your wages have been garnished for more than one debt.

If the employer violates the law, he may be subject to a fine of up to $1,000.00 and imprisonment of up to one year, or both. You may also file a *civil action* against the employer.

Wage garnishments under federal law are regulated by the U.S. Department of Labor.

Non-Wage Garnishments

The judgment creditor may also garnish other money due to you, such as checking account balances and savings accounts. When a bank is served with a garnishment directed at a depositor's account, the bank is not required to determine the depositor's right to a wage earner's exemption under the Consumer Credit Act, the Restriction on Garnishment provisions of the Code of Federal Regulations, or applicable state statutes, and is not required to calculate the amount of the exemption before honoring the garnishment. In other words, the entire account, or the amount required to satisfy the judgment, can be garnished.

WRIT OF EXECUTION AND LEVY

The judgment against you may have to be recorded in the public records before the creditor can take any further action.

Example: It may not be sufficient for a creditor to get a judgment against you in order for that judgment to appear as a lien against your real property. The judgment may also have to be filed in the county recorder's office.

NOTE: *If the creditor obtained his judgment in another state or county, there may be certain procedural requirements the creditor must meet in order for the judgment to be valid where the creditor is attempting to collect it.*

If a judgment creditor attempts to attach property, you should determine whether the judgment was properly recorded. If not, you may have a defense to enforcement of the order authorizing the attachment (at least temporarily).

Upon the request of the judgment creditor, the court can enter an order (often included in the final judgment) granting a writ of execution. The writ of execution serves as a lien against your property, and is good through the life of the judgment. (Judgments remain as liens on your property for three to twenty years, depending upon the state in which the judgment was entered. Most are valid between ten and twenty years.)

The property subject to the writ of execution may include property acquired *after* the writ of execution has been signed by the court. (In other words, property you get *after* the judgment is entered may also be taken to pay the judgment amount.) The writ of execution may also contain instructions to the sheriff or other law enforcement officials to levy or take the property identified in the writ of execution. A *levy* is the absolute legal taking of the property levied on for the payment of a judgment debt. (There is a sample of a writ on page 180. Although the form used in your particular state may vary somewhat, the intent remains the same.)

The sheriff is required to take as much property as is necessary to satisfy the judgment. Except for real estate, the sheriff must take the property into his possession. If the sheriff breaks into your residence to take the property, he should have a court order to do so. Otherwise, he can only enter your residence peacefully (with your consent).

The property is then sold, and the proceeds used to pay the judgment. To avoid the levy, the law may allow you to make payment in full on the writ. As mentioned above, you can also appeal to the court explaining that the property is essential for your livelihood. Once the property is taken, then the sheriff is responsible for its loss or destruction.

Forced sale of certain property will be prohibited by law if the property is exempt (see Chapter 16).

ATTACHMENT OF PROPERTY NOT YET IN YOUR POSSESSION

The judgment creditor can ask the court for an order allowing him to intercept property that would otherwise come to you, such as a tax refund, commissions, or royalties. You must be given notice of the hearing and you have the right to explain to the court why the order should not be entered. If it is ordered in spite of your efforts, then a copy is sent to the person holding the property, such as your real estate broker or publisher, and the payments are then made directly to the judgment creditor.

ATTACHMENT OF PROPERTY BEFORE JUDGMENT

An *attachment* is a special proceeding authorizing a creditor to take your property *before* he or she gets a judgment. It is granted if the creditor believes you will attempt to delay the court proceedings for collection, that you will move the assets out of reach of the creditor, or that you have an intent to defraud the creditor.

Under normal circumstances a creditor may not attach your property without first obtaining a judgment and then a writ of execution as described previously. However, if the creditor has reason to believe that the property will be removed from the court's reach, the court may order the property to be attached.

Example: The sellers of a restaurant sued the buyers for breach of contract, but no final judgment had yet been ordered by the court. The sellers were able to have the buyers' property attached for the reason that the buyers were about to leave the state.

In order to take your property before a judgment is entered:

- the creditor must post a bond;

- the creditor must file an affidavit with the court stating why the property should be attached; and

- a writ of attachment must be issued by a court of law.

To avoid having your property attached, you also have an opportunity to post a *bond* that will pay the judgment amount if in fact a judgment is entered. After the property is attached, there must be a hearing at which the grounds for the attachment must be proven by the creditor. If you can prove to the court that you are not intending to move the property from the court's reach, that you are not intending to move from the state, and that you have no intention of defrauding your creditor, then the court should release the writ of attachment.

The legal procedure where property is taken before a judgment is actually entered must be carefully followed by a creditor. As a debtor, you may have a defense that the constitutional requirements of due process were not met before the property was taken. (The due process requirements include the filing of the creditor's affidavit with the court, the filing of a bond by the creditor, the issuance by the court of a writ of attachment, and the opportunity for the debtor to post a bond.)

FOR FURTHER RESEARCH

Read your state's statutes regarding the legal procedure for collection of a judgment, including garnishment, levy, and attachment, noting the maximum time periods allowed for the various steps in the process. When you research your state's statutes, ask the librarian for an *annotated* version. This will include cases that might help clarify certain provisions of the law. The cases will also give you an idea of what kinds of defenses other people in situations similar to yours have presented to the court.

The federal exemptions from garnishment are found in United States Code Annotated, Title 15, Chapter 41, Subchapter II, Restrictions on Garnishment, Sections 1671 through 1677.

EXAMPLE: WRIT OF GARNISHMENT

IN THE CIRCUIT COURT OF THE _____ JUDICIAL CIRCUIT
IN AND FOR _____ COUNTY, _____

Plaintiff

vs.   Case No.

Defendant
(your name)

GARNISHMENT
WRIT OF GARNISHMENT

THE STATE OF _____

To each Sheriff of the State:

YOU ARE COMMANDED to summon garnishee, ____(employer)__to serve an answer to this writ on _____(plaintiff's attorney) whose address is _____, within days after service on the garnishee, exclusive of the day of service, and to file the original with the clerk of this court either before service on the attorney or immediately thereafter, stating whether the garnishee is indebted to defendant, (your name)___ at the time of the answer or was indebted at the time of service of the writ, or at any time between such times, and in what amount, and what tangible and intangible personal property of the defendant the garnishee has in his possession or control at the time of the answer or had at the time of service of this writ, or at any time between such times, and whether the garnishee knows of any other person indebted to the defendant or who may have any of the property of the defendant in his possession or control. The amount set in plaintiff's motion is $_____.

Dated _____

Signed by the Court Clerk

BANKRUPTCY AS AN OPTION

14

Bankruptcy is a legal and legitimate method of wiping out most, if not all, of your debts. Bankruptcy laws can be traced back hundreds of years. Bankruptcy is usually considered a last resort for credit problems, but if there is no foreseeable change in your income and you are likely to lose everything because of insurmountable debt, then it may be your best alternative.

The bankruptcy laws were enacted to give people overwhelmed with debt an opportunity for a fresh start, and if you are at the point of considering bankruptcy as a real possibility, then you should keep this in mind. It is also important to note that only certain debts, commonly referred to as *unsecured debts*, can be eliminated by a bankruptcy proceeding. The two most common are debts related to medical treatments and credit cards. However, in some cases even credit card debts will not be discharged in bankruptcy, particularly if used excessively shortly before filing bankruptcy.

Some companies such as Sears issue secured credit cards. In other words, Sears has a security interest in the property you are purchasing using the card and subject to the bankruptcy procedures, can take property back if you fail to pay.

NOTE: *At the time of this printing, the United States Congress is currently working on a new bankruptcy law that is expected to be signed by the President this year. It will make it more difficult for people (and in some cases businesses) to discharge their debts.*

The income and necessary expenses of applicants will be scrutinized. For example, those who will have enough income to pay at least 25% of their debts over five years will be required to file under Chapter 13 instead of Chapter 7. If allowed to file under Chapter 7, individuals will be required to complete a credit-counseling program.

You should keep in mind as you read this chapter that substantial changes to the filing requirements and exemptions are anticipated.

Other than the exempt property used to pay current debts, the law assumes you have no resources when you file for bankruptcy.

Example: If you own a vehicle worth $8,000, and the exemption allowed by your state is $1,000, then the bankruptcy court will require that the vehicle be sold and used to pay your unsecured debts. In this case, the loss of your property may not be worth using the bankruptcy process to eliminate your debt.

Congress, in the Bankruptcy Reform Act of 1994, also made it more difficult for an ex-spouse to use bankruptcy to eliminate debts resulting from a property settlement agreement. However, the exception to discharge only applies if the ex-spouse has the ability to pay and the detriment to the other spouse outweighs the fresh-start benefit of bankruptcy. Alimony and child support are priority debts that must be paid first.

If a credit card was used to pay income taxes, the credit card debt cannot then be eliminated through bankruptcy.

TYPES OF BANKRUPTCY

There are several types of bankruptcies for individuals: Chapter 7, Chapter 11, and Chapter 13. Bankruptcy under Chapter 7 discharges your debts, and at the end of the process you are debt-free. Chapter 11 bankruptcy allows you to act as your own trustee and reorganize your debts. Bankruptcy under Chapter 13, sometimes called a *wage earners bankruptcy*, allows you to work out a payment plan whereby you pay back your creditors all or part of the amount you owe them over a period of time.

Bankruptcy, while it will not necessarily terminate foreclosure proceedings, can give you months (sometimes years) before you actually lose your property. Even if you file one day before the foreclosure sale, the process is immediately stopped. The lender can ask the bankruptcy court to allow the foreclosure to proceed—you still have the claims and defenses available to you as detailed in Chapter 10.

HOW BANKRUPTCY WORKS

All bankruptcies are handled by the U.S. Bankruptcy Court. (There should be a U.S. Bankruptcy Court in your Federal Court district.) A petition for bankruptcy is filed, creditors are notified, and the process begins. Following are the general procedures for each type of case.

Chapter 7

Under Chapter 7, your assets are generally liquidated to pay the creditors. When the petition in bankruptcy court is filed, all creditors are notified. Once notified, the creditor *cannot* contact you directly about your debt, but must file a claim with the bankruptcy trustee. The creditor *cannot* file a lawsuit against you after receiving notice of your bankruptcy, nor can the creditor continue to pursue any existing lawsuit.

Trustee. The bankruptcy trustee appointed by the court will hold a meeting of your creditors to allow the creditors to ask questions regarding the debt owed to them. The trustee will also take all of your assets over and above those you are allowed by law to keep (*exempt* assets), and sell them. The proceeds of the sale will be used to pay the trustee for his or her services, any administrative expenses, and ultimately your creditors. (In most cases there is no money left to pay the creditors.) If there are no objections to your bankruptcy filed with the court, an order will then be entered discharging you from all your debts.

If you do not cooperate with the bankruptcy trustee or comply with a court order, or if your debts are consumer debts and you could pay them off with modest effort between three to five years, then your request for a discharge may be denied by the court. However, as a practical matter most people who file under Chapter 7 are granted a discharge in bankruptcy.

Chapter 13

Under Chapter 13, creditors are also notified and must stop all action against you to collect their debts. (If your unsecured debts total more than $268,250, and secured debts more than $807,750, you will not be eligible to file under Chapter 13.) You must work out a payment plan for your creditors, proposing to pay back all or a pro rata share of the amount due them. The repayment should include your mortgage and tax bills. All of your creditors must agree to the repayment plan. Once you have made all of the payments according to your plan, the court will discharge you from those debts.

Chapter 11

Until a 1991 U. S. Supreme Court Ruling, only business entities could file under Chapter 11, but now it can be applied to individuals. Unlike Chapters 7 or 13, a trustee is not automatically appointed, and you can remain in control of your property with the duties and powers exercised by a trustee under Chapters 7 and 13. Filing under Chapter 11 requires a plan to organize your debts, and allows you to continue your business operation.

BANKRUPTCY AND ELIMINATION OF DEBTS

Bankruptcy will not eliminate all of your debts. The following is a list of debts that are not *dischargeable* (i.e. from which you can be relieved from payment) in bankruptcy:

- Any recent debts owed to the Internal Revenue Service;

- most alimony or child support payment orders;

- obligations owed as a result of criminal or fraudulent actions;

- certain types of student loans;

- income taxes less than three years past due;

- court judgments resulting in damages due to your driving while intoxicated;

- any payroll taxes that you failed to pay as a responsible person in a business; and

- a debt owed to any creditor you fail to notify of the bankruptcy.

THE BANKRUPTCY COURT AND YOUR PROPERTY

Under the federal bankruptcy law and state laws certain property is exempt and cannot be used by the trustee to satisfy your creditors. These exemptions vary from state to state. However, your state exemptions may apply in lieu of the federal bankruptcy exceptions.

The federal bankruptcy law exemptions may be used in Arkansas, Connecticut, Hawaii, Massachusetts, Michigan, Minnesota, New Jersey, New Mexico, Pennsylvania, Rhode Island, Texas, Vermont, Washington, and Wisconsin. These states also have their own exemptions, but you need to decide whether the federal or state exemptions will allow you to keep more of your property. If you do not live in one of the states listed above, you can only use your state law exemptions. As of April 1, 2001 the adjusted federal bankruptcy exemptions were:

- your right to receive:

- a social security benefit, unemployment compensation, or local public assistance benefit;
- a veteran's benefit;
- a disability, illness or unemployment benefit;
- alimony, support, or separate maintenance payments to the extent reasonably necessary for you and/or your dependents' support;
- a payment under a stock bonus, pension, profit-sharing, annuity, or similar plan or contract on account of illness, disability, death, age, or length of service, to the extent reasonably necessary for you and/or your dependents' support, unless
  1. the plan or contract was established by someone who employed you at the time your rights under the plan accrued;
  2. the plan is on account of your age and length of service; and
  3. the plan doesn't qualify under certain provisions of the Internal Revenue Code;
- your homestead, including a mobile home or cooperative apartment, to the extent of $16,150.00;
- any unused portion of the $16,150.00 homestead exemption to the extent of $8,075 may be applied to any other property up to $850 in value;
- personal property including clothing, appliances, furnishings, household goods to $425 each and a total of $8,625;

- tools of trade (for use in your business) to the extent of $1,625;
- a motor vehicle to the extent of $2,575;
- wrongful death recoveries for a person you depended on;
- personal injury awards to the extent of $16, 150 (plus damages for pain and suffering and dollar loss);
- jewelry to $1,075;
- health aids;
- crime victims compensation;
- life insurance policy with loan value in accrued dividends or interest up to $8,625; and
- unmatured life insurance contract, except credit insurance policy.

(The exemption amounts are adjusted every three years.)

Only payments reasonably necessary for support are exempt. The bankruptcy law is concerned with your present, not future, security, and thus will generally not exempt savings plans unless you are receiving current income from them.

If you use your state's exemptions, then you may also use these federal non-bankruptcy exemptions:

- retirement benefits as follows: social security, veteran's benefits, railroad workers benefits, military service employee benefits, military honor roll pensions, foreign service employee pensions, civil service and CIA employee benefits;
- survivor's benefits of U.S. judges, court directors, judicial center directors, supreme court chief justice administrators;

- death and disability benefits for military service, war risk hazard injury or death compensation; or

- miscellaneous benefits such as military group life insurance, the greater of 75% of your weekly net income or $114.00 per week, military deposits into a savings account while you are on permanent duty outside the United States, railroad workers unemployment insurance, and seaman's contract wages while at sea.

State homestead and garnishment exemptions are discussed more in the next chapter of this book.

In a Chapter 7 case, you may decide that you need your car or other property on which you owe money. Rather than have the creditor take the property and have the bankruptcy court discharge your debt to that creditor, you may be able to *reaffirm* that particular debt. By reaffirming the debt, you are making a commitment to that creditor that you will continue the payments. Both the creditor and the bankruptcy trustee must approve your request to reaffirm any debt.

PROS AND CONS

Opinions vary as to the effect of a discharge in bankruptcy. Most experts agree that bankruptcy should be used only as a last resort, primarily because of the negative effect it may have on your credit record. The bankruptcy filing will stay in the credit reporting agency's file for a period of ten years. If you are at the point of considering bankruptcy, then your credit report probably is not very high on your list of priorities.

The primary concern of most people who are considering bankruptcy is the inability to get credit after discharge. However, with the large number of bankruptcy filings, some lenders are changing their attitudes. Once all your debts are discharged, you have that much more disposable income to repay a loan. The fact that you have more money available and cannot file Chapter 7 bankruptcy again for another six years may provide the lender a certain level of comfort in giving you a loan.

Finally, many individuals and businesses are now filing for protection from creditors under the bankruptcy laws. Although feelings of guilt and failure are often associated with bankruptcy, remember that the primary purpose of the law is to provide a fresh start.

HOW TO FILE FOR BANKRUPTCY

You can file for bankruptcy with the assistance of an attorney. The attorney's fee must be disclosed in the bankruptcy petition. You can also file for bankruptcy on your own. Before attempting to file your own bankruptcy, you should familiarize yourself with the forms and procedures.

FOR FURTHER RESEARCH

The full text of the bankruptcy laws are found at United States Code, Title 11. The exemptions are found at United States Code, Title 11, Section 522.

DIVORCE, DEBT, AND COMMUNITY PROPERTY 15

Marriage is typically the joyful and hopeful union of two people, and most often the union of their assets as well as their financial obligations. Situations involving pre-nuptial agreements are beyond the scope of this book. The smiling couple plans to buy a house, have children, and live happily ever after. Divorce, on the other hand, is often an emotionally and financially devastating experience.

Marriage and Debt

Most couples begin their married lives by opening up joint bank accounts, signing jointly on leases, mortgages, and car loans, and applying for credit in both names. This joint effort may help in obtaining credit that either one of the parties on his or her own would not be able to get. When a joint credit account is opened, the assets, credit history, and income of both parties are combined and considered by a prospective creditor. On the other hand, both parties are then responsible for repayment of any credit extended on a joint application.

For credit reporting purposes, the account history must be reported in both names. Each spouse is fully liable.

Of course, each spouse can maintain an individual account as well, which will not be affected by the other spouse's credit. (Except in community property states as discussed later.) If an individual account holder authorizes another to use the credit (for example, a gasoline credit card given by a parent to a student), the account holder, not the user, is responsible for repayment. For credit reporting purposes, a credit report is issued both in the account holder's and the authorized user's name.

PROPERTY SETTLEMENTS AND COURT JUDGMENTS

If the marriage ends in divorce, division of debt can become at least as important an issue as division of assets. Many times a divorce settlement or court judgment will set forth which party is responsible for payment of which obligations. The separated or divorced spouses rely on such a document, assuming they are no longer liable for the debt, and are surprised when contacted by a creditor for payment. However, neither a settlement agreement nor a court judgment will relieve a spouse of any debt jointly entered into with the other spouse.

Family Residence
If your former spouse kept the family residence and agreed to make the mortgage payments, you may have given him or her a *quitclaim deed* and assumed that you had no further liability. However, if you have any doubt about his or her financial reli-

ability, you should consider checking periodically to make sure the payments are current. If the lender forecloses, you will be named in the lawsuit as a defendant since you are still obligated on the mortgage.

Credit Rating

To minimize the risk of losing your good credit rating or finding yourself unable to meet financial obligations because your former spouse may fail to pay the debts that were assumed by him or her in divorce, you might be better off selling as many of your joint assets as possible to pay off the liabilities. In exceptional situations a creditor might be willing to let you off the hook; for example, if your spouse puts up more collateral for repayment. You might also be able to take a security interest in the property transferred to your former spouse, which will be released when the debts are paid. This would provide you with an asset to sell should the creditor come to you for payment. On real estate, require that your former spouse obtain a new mortgage in his or her own name, and that the mortgage in joint names be paid in full.

DEBT ASSUMED IN DIVORCE

A property settlement agreement with your ex-spouse does not relieve you of any debt you jointly obligated yourselves to pay. If, for example, you and your ex-spouse used a joint credit card, you will both be held liable for payment. A property settlement agreement may specifically spell out which spouse will take over payment of certain bills. However, if your former spouse fails to make the payments as required under your agreement, the creditor will look to you for the money. You can argue that by agreement he or she is responsible for the debt. Unless the creditor released you from any obligation to pay, you may still be held responsible.

Example: Bruce had been divorced for over a year and was planning to remarry. Before his remarriage he received notice that his former wife had filed bankruptcy, thereby eliminating her obligation on the debts she had agreed to pay. The property settlement Bruce had reached with her, which was filed in the court records, described each debt and which party would accept responsibility for payment. However, the creditors had not released Bruce, and when his wife filed for bankruptcy they looked to Bruce for payment. Bruce was able to manage fine with his portion of the debt as divided in the settlement agreement, but was unable to carry his former spouse's financial obligations as well. Bruce filed for Chapter 7 bankruptcy.

This is also true of your day-to-day service providers.

NOTE: *The Bankruptcy Reform Act of 1994 makes it more difficult, but not impossible, for an ex-spouse to eliminate debt owed under a Property Settlement Agreement. If you believe your ex-spouse has the ability to pay, you should file an exception to the bankruptcy proceeding. (See Chapter 14.)*

Example: Even if your former spouse has agreed to pay your child's medical bills, you may be held responsible. If you take your child for medical treatment, the physician will most likely look to you for payment. The physician is not a party to any agreement you may have with a former spouse.

If possible, you should make advance arrangements with your former spouse and the service provider for payment of these types of bills, so that ultimately non-payment will not have a negative effect on your credit report.

Quit Claim Deed

Finally, if your former spouse kept the family residence and agreed to make the mortgage payments, you may have given him or her a *quitclaim deed* and assumed that you had no further liability. However, if you have any doubt about his or her financial reliability, you should consider checking periodically to make sure the payments are current. If the lender forecloses, then you will be named in the lawsuit as a defendant since you are still obligated on the mortgage.

COMMUNITY PROPERTY AND DEBT

The states of Alaska, Arizona, California, Idaho, Louisiana, Nevada, New Mexico, Texas, Washington and Wisconsin have some type of "community property" legislation. Community property describes the unique property interests of husband and wife under these states' laws. For example, income earned by one spouse may be considered community property. That is, property belonging to both husband and wife. Typically all property of either spouse, regardless of how it is titled (individually or as "husband and wife") is considered community property unless proven otherwise (separate property must be defined in a contract or proven to be separate), and includes all property acquired during the marriage by either spouse, any income from and increase in value to any such property), and any property purchased from income earned during the marriage. If a business owned by one spouse before marriage increases in value during the marriage, the increase may be considered community property. Both spouses have the full right to manage and control the community property, including any sales, leases, gifts, etc. In some cases a marriage contract can be entered into, which supercedes the community property laws.

In community property states, generally all debts incurred during a marriage, regardless by which spouse, are considered *community debts*. Even if only one spouse signs, these are debts viewed as for the benefit of community of both spouses, or for the benefit of the other spouse. (An exception exists if the spouses have either by contract or otherwise defined their separate property, however, the spouse not incurring the debt may still be liable to the extent of any benefit received from the debt.)

Example: If the husband purchases a dishwasher, and signs the financing agreement without the co-signature of his wife, his wife may still be held liable because the dishwasher benefitted both spouses.

Separate Property
Even if the spouses have clearly identified separate property, the separate property can be used to satisfy a debt that was otherwise designated a community debt–both husband and wife received a benefit from the debt. Although various

aspects of debt incurred during a marriage may be different under community property laws, the same suggestions in dealing with creditors apply as in non-community property states.

THE INNOCENT SPOUSE AND THE IRS

Most married taxpayers file a joint income tax return; in some cases one spouse will sign, unaware of the details contained in the return or the financial dealings of the other spouse. Even so, the innocent spouse can be held liable for the money due to the Internal Revenue Service, regardless of whether you have been separated or divorced in the meantime. The new tax law, known as Innocent Spouse Relief, (in addition to Separation of Liability and Equitable Relief) attempts to assist spouses who, in spite of the fact that they signed the tax return, were totally unaware of any unreported income, incorrect deductions, credits, or other irregularities which resulted in assessment of additional taxes, and who did not knowingly benefit from any such irregularities.

Assistance is also available if you filed a joint tax return, and the IRS took your refund to satisfy your spouse's or former spouse's past due tax, a federal debt such as a student loan, or child support. Because community income and expenses are attributed equally to both husband and wife in community property states, a special provision exists for assistance to spouses in those states.

To obtain relief, one of several different forms, depending upon the situation, must be filed with the IRS. Detailed information about the forms and circumstances in which it is appropriate to file are found in IRS Publication 971. Publication 971, and the forms, are available on the IRS website, **http://www.irs.ustreas.gov/** or call 800-829-1040.

PROPERTY EXEMPT FROM CREDITORS 16

As explained in Chapter 14, the Bankruptcy Act prohibits certain property (exempt property) from being taken by the bankruptcy trustee to satisfy your debts. (In a bankruptcy, either your state or the bankruptcy Act exemptions will apply.) In other words, you will be able to keep the exempt property even though you have filed for and been discharged by the bankruptcy court.

There are also federal and state laws that exempt certain property from judgment creditors. In this case, *exempt property* is property that a creditor will not be able to take to satisfy a judgment even if you do not file for bankruptcy. The federal exemptions that you may claim, (except for seaman's clothing), involve strictly monetary benefits. The federal non-bankruptcy exemptions are set forth in Chapter 14 of this book.

The state exemptions may include your homestead (most states allow only a certain portion of the equity to be exempt), a specified portion of your wages, pension and unemployment benefits, public assistance, insurance benefits, tools you must use in your business, and a certain amount of personal property. In some states, if property is owned by you *and* your spouse, and a judgment is entered against only one of you, the jointly-owned property may be unavailable to judgment creditors. (A number of states recognize *tenancy by the entirety* property owned by husband and wife, which is usually exempt from the creditors of only one spouse. See "Homestead Exemptions" beginning on page 202.)

You should be aware of and understand your state's exemptions to determine exactly what property may be taken from you for the payment of debts. (California has two alternative lists of exemptions.) You will need this information in order to complete the personal financial assessment in the next chapter. Also, property given as collateral for a loan is not exempt to the extent of the loan, even though it might be listed as an exemption in your state.

Two of the most important exemptions available—your home and your wages—are listed at the end of this chapter state by state. Information about additional exemptions available in your state may be obtained at your local library or the state attorney's office. (Most are included in the statutes listed immediately below the name of your state on the lists on pages 202-213.) Remember that the homestead exemption protects your equity in the property to the dollar amount specified by law in your particular state—it does not protect you against foreclosure of a mortgage or loan for which the property was given as collateral.

You should also check with your local court clerk or recorder's office whether or not you must record a statement in the public records listing your exempt property and claiming the exemption, and whether your statement must be published. If at all possible you should be sure that any required filing is done *before* a lawsuit is filed against you or your property is attached. (A sample declaration of homestead used in Florida is included at the end of this chapter on page 214.)

If you are in doubt as to whether property a creditor is trying to take from you is exempt, go ahead and assert the exemption as a defense. If the creditor contests your claim, the court will decide. It is better to make the attempt and be refused an exemption, than to allow the creditor to take property you should be able to keep.

STATE-BY-STATE HOMESTEAD EXEMPTIONS

Your *homestead* is your dwelling, with its land and buildings occupied by you as a home, and exempted by law from seizure or sale for a debt. The extent of the homestead varies from state to state. For a more detailed explanation, you should read the statute section referenced below your state's name.

In addition, your state may be one that recognizes title held by a husband and wife as tenants by the entireties. If so, it is likely that, as to the property to which title is held in that manner, the property will be exempt from collection for the debts of only one spouse. Among the states that recognize tenants by the entireties are: Florida, Massachusetts, Indiana, Missouri, Ohio, Tennessee, Vermont, and Virginia. (Be sure to check your state's statutes.)

Alabama Sec. 6-10-2	$5,000 value property, up to 160 acres each (separate exemptions for husband and wife) 320 acres total for husband and wife.
Alaska Sec. 9.38.010	Value to $54,000 based upon percentage ownership in the property; if more than one owner, the aggregate exemptions for one living unit cannot exceed $54,000.
Arizona Secs. 33-1101, 33-1101(c)	$100,000 in real property, apartment or mobile home plus land; if you sell, proceeds are exempt for up to 18 months.
Arkansas Constitution Secs. 9-3 & 9-5, 16-66-210	For head of family, unlimited value; 1 acre (not to be reduced to less than 1/4 acre in town), 160 acres (not to be reduced to less than 80 acres) elsewhere, $2,500 value. For others, $800 if single, $1,250 if married. (If in city, 160 acres still applies if property remains rural in nature.)

California Secs. 704.720, 704.730, 703.140(b)(1)	Property to $50,000 if not disabled & single; $75,000 for families if no other member has a homestead; $100,000 if 65 or older, mentally or physically disabled; $100,000 if 55 or older, single & earn under $15,000 or married and earn under $20,000 and creditors force sale of home. Sale proceeds are exempt for six months. (California has two alternative exemption lists—the second list exempts real or personal property to $7,500.)
Colorado Secs. 38-41-201, 38-41-201.6, 13-54-102.5	Real property to $30,000, trailer $3,500, mobile home $6,000, sale proceeds exempt. (spouse or child of deceased may claim homestead exemption
Connecticut Sec. 52-352(b)	Real property or mobile home up to $75,000.
Delaware Sec. 10.4901	None (some personal articles exempt).(however, real property held by married couples may be exempt against debts owed by one spouse)
District of **Columbia**	None.
Florida Sec. 222.05, Const., Art. 10-4	Unlimited value; up to 1/2 acre in a municipality and 160 acres elsewhere.(tenants by the entirety property exempt against debt of only one spouse)
Georgia Sec. 44-13-100	Interest in property used as residence to $5,000, including co-op.
Hawaii Secs. 36-651-91&92, 651-96	Cannot exceed one acre. Head of household or over age 65, value to $30,000; all others, $20,000. Proceeds exempt for six months.
Idaho Secs. 55-1003, 55-1004	Lesser of $50,000 value, or total net value of all lands, mobile home improvements; sale proceeds exempt for six months.

Illinois
Secs. 110-12-901,
110-12-906

Property occupied as residence value to
$7,500; sale proceeds exempt for one year.

Indiana
Secs.34-2-28-1,
1(a) & 1(b)

Value to $7,500 for each debtor; homestead
and personal property exemptions can't
exceed $10,000.

Iowa
Secs. 499A.18,
561.2 & 561.16

Within city, 1/2 acre, 40 acres elsewhere.

Kansas
Sec. 60-2301
Const., Art.15-9

Unlimited value; 1 acre in town, 160 acres
elsewhere.

Kentucky
Secs. 427-060,
427-090

Property value to $5,000; sale proceeds
exempt

Louisiana
Sec. 20:1

Value to $15,000; maximum 160 acres on
one tract, or two or more tracts if home on
one and field, garden or pasture on others.

Maine
Sec. 14-4422

Value to $12,500 (includes burial plot); if
you are 60 or over, or mentally or physically
disabled (unable to work for at least 12
months) to $60,000, if living with minors, to
$25,000.

Maryland

None, $15,500 in wild card exemptions

Massachusetts
Sec. 188-1, 1A

Value to $300,000. If over 62, $200,000, provided an elderly or disabled persons declaration of homestead protection is filed with
supporting documentation.

Michigan
Secs. MCLA 600.1823,
559.214, 700.285

Value to $3,500; 1 lot in town, 40 acres else-
where.

Minnesota
Secs. 510.01 & .02,
550.37

1/2 acre in town, 160 acres elsewhere (mobile home included), to $200,000, or to $500,000 if for agricultural use; proceeds are exempt.

Mississippi
Sec. 85-3-21
Miss Const., Sec. 94

Value to $75,000; to 160 acres; sale proceeds exempt.

Missouri
Secs. 513.430,
513.475,
513.430(6)

Real property value to $8,000; mobile home used as principal residence, to $1,000.

Montana
Secs. 70-32-101 &
70-32-104,
25-13-614

Value to $60,000; sale proceeds exempt 18 months; 1/4 acre in town, 320 acres outside.

Nebraska
Secs. 40-101,
40-113

Value to $10,000; maximum 2 lots in city, 160 acres elsewhere.

Nevada
Secs.21.090(M),
21.090(E),
115.010

Value to $125,000 exempt.

Real property to $30,000.

New Hampshire
Sec. 480:1

None.

New Jersey
Sec. 2A:17-17

Real property to $30,000 if married, widowed or supporting another (if jointly owned, exemption may be doubled).

New Mexico
Sec. 42-10-9

New York
Civil Practice
Law & Rules,
5206

Real property, co-op, condo or mobile home value to $10,000; husband and wife can double exemption.

North Carolina Sec. 1C-1601 Const., Art. X-2	Value to $10,000 in a residence.
North Dakota Secs. 47-18-01, 47-18-14	Value to $80,000. Proceeds exempt.
Ohio Sec. 2329.66	Residence value to $5,000.
Oklahoma Secs. 31-2(1), 31-2(2), 31-2	$5,000 on one acre in city or on 160 acres (one or more parcels) elsewhere (not to be reduced to less than 1/4 acre regardless of value.
Oregon Secs. 23.164, 23.164(1), 23.164(5), 23.250, 23.240, 23.242	$25,000 ($33,000 if joint ownership); $23,000 ($30,000 if joint ownership) for mobile home & land; if land not owned, mobile home exemption (includes "houseboat") is $20,000 ($27,000 if joint ownership); land limited to 1 block in city, 160 acres elsewhere; sale proceeds exempt 1 year if buying another home.
Pennsylvania	None.
Rhode Island	None.
South Carolina Sec. 15-41-30	Residence value to $5,000 (Aggregate of multiple exemptions on same property is $10,000).
South Dakota Sec. 43-31-1,2&4	Real property to unlimited value, including mobile home if 240 or more square feet and registered 6 mos. before claim of exemption; 1 acre in town, 160 elsewhere; proceeds to $30,000 (unlimited if over age 70) exempt for 1 year.

Tennessee Sec. 26-2-301	Value to $5,000; $7,500 if joint ownership (to be equally divided if there are simultaneous claims).
Texas Secs. 41.001 & .002	Unlimited value; 1 acre in town, 100 acres (200 if family) elsewhere; sale proceeds exempt for 6 months.
Utah Sec. 78-23-3	Property to value of $10,000; $20,000 if joint.
Vermont Sec. T.27-101	Residence and land value to $30,000.
Virginia Sec. 34-4	Property value to $5,000, plus $500 for each dependent; additional exemption for certain veterans.
Washington Secs. 6.13.010 & .180	Property value to $30,000; proceeds exempt.
West Virginia Secs. 38-10-4, 38-9-3	Residence value to $5,000.
Wisconsin Sec. 815.20	Residence value to $40,000; sale proceeds exempt for 2 years if you're buying another home.
Wyoming Secs. 1-20-101 & 104	Residence value to $10,000; house trailer to $6,000.

STATE-BY-STATE GARNISHMENT EXEMPTIONS

Wages are payments for services rendered by an individual. For the purposes of determining the amount of your wage exemption, generally only the amount of your *disposable* (after tax and withholding) earnings are considered wages. The information provided below is merely a brief outline. The amount or percentage shown is that amount that is exempt from garnishment (i.e. not available to creditors to satisfy a debt.)

Where the exempt amount is based upon a multiple of the federal minimum hourly wage (U.S.C.,Title 29, Section 106 (a)(1)), and you are paid on other than a weekly basis, the multiples must be adjusted based upon your pay period. Please note that in cases where wages are being garnished for money due under a support order, the exempt amount may be substantially reduced (a larger amount will be available to the creditor).

You should read your state statute shown below the state name to help you in calculating the exact amount of your wage exemption, and for a listing of other income and property which may be beyond the reach of your creditors.

Alabama
Sec. 6-10-7

75% of your weekly wage, salary or compensation is exempt.

Alaska
Secs. 9.38.030,
9.38.050,
938.015,
938.025

Weekly net earnings to $350; for sole household wage earner, $550. If you don't get paid monthly, semi-monthly or weekly, then you can claim $1,400 in cash or liquid assets paid in any month; the sole wage earner can claim $2,200; including disability benefits.

Arizona
Sec. 33-1131(B)

Either 75% of your weekly net earnings or 30 times the Federal minimum hourly wage, whichever is greater, is exempt (only half are exempt if the garnishment is for support).

Arkansas
Sec. 16-66-208

Any earned but unpaid wages due for 60 days, but $25 per week is absolutely exempt.

California
Secs. 704.113,
704.070

75% of your wages paid within 30 days before a writ is issued are exempt, (all wages are exempt if before payment they were subject to a withholding order or wage assignment for support).

Colorado
Sec. 13-54-104

Either 75% of your weekly net earnings or 30 times the Federal minimum hourly wage, whichever is greater, is exempt.

Connecticut
Sec. 52-361(a)

Either 75% of your weekly net earnings or 40 times the Federal minimum hourly wage, whichever is greater, is exempt.

Delaware
Sec. 10-4913

85% of your unpaid wages or other remuneration.

District of Columbia
Sec. 16-572

Either 75% of your weekly net earnings or 30 times the Federal minimum hourly wage, whichever is greater, is exempt.

Florida
Sec. 222.11

Wages are exempt if head of household.

Georgia
Secs.18-4-20,
18-4-21

Either 75% of your weekly net earnings or 30 times the Federal minimum hourly wage, whichever is greater, is exempt.

Hawaii
Sec. 36-651-121

95% of 1st $100, 90% of 2nd $100, 80% of net wages in excess of $200 per month or federal limits, whichever is greater.

209

Idaho Sec. 11-207	Either 75% of your weekly net earnings or 30 times the Federal minimum hourly wage, whichever is greater, is exempt.
Illinois Sec. 110-12-803	Either 85% of your weekly net earnings or 45 times the Federal minimum hourly wage, whichever is greater, is exempt.
Indiana Secs. 24-4.5-5-105 2(a) & (b)	Either 75% of your weekly net earnings or 30 times the Federal minimum hourly wage, whichever is greater, is exempt.
Iowa Sec. 642.21	75% of disposable earnings per week or an amount equal to 30 x the federal minimum wage, whichever is greater.
Kansas Sec. 60-2310	Either 75% of your weekly net earnings or 30 times the Federal minimum hourly wage, whichever is greater, is exempt.
Kentucky Sec. 427.010	Either 75% of your weekly net earnings or 30 times the Federal minimum hourly wage, whichever is greater, is exempt.
Louisiana Sec. 13.3881	Either 75% of your weekly net earnings or 30 times the Federal minimum hourly wage, whichever is greater, is exempt.
Maine Sec. 14-3127(1)	Either 75% of your weekly net earnings or 40 times the Federal minimum hourly wage, whichever is greater, is exempt.
Maryland Sec. 15-601.1	Either 75% of your weekly net earnings or 30 times the Federal minimum hourly wage, whichever is greater, is exempt in Caroline, Kent, Queen Anne and Worcester Counties; in other counties, greater of 75% of actual wages or $145 per week.
Massachusetts Sec. c.246-28	Pension payments being received by Trustee. Unpaid but earned wages up to $125 per week (held by Trustee) are exempt.

Michigan
Sec. 600-5311

75% of disposable earnings per week or an amount equal to 30 x the federal minimum hourly wage, whichever is greater.

Minnesota
Sec. 571.55(2)

Either 75% of your weekly net earnings or 40 times the Federal minimum hourly wage, whichever is greater, is exempt .

Mississippi
Sec. 85 3-4(2)

An amount equal to 30 x the federal minimum hourly wage.

Missouri
Sec. 525.030

Either 90% of your weekly net earnings or an amount equal to 30 x the federal minimum hourly wage, whichever is greater.

Montana
Sec. 25-13-614

Either 75% of your weekly net earnings or 30 times the Federal minimum hourly wage, whichever is greater, is exempt.

Nebraska
Sec. 25-1558

Either 75% (85% for head of household) of your weekly net earnings or 30 times the Federal minimum hourly wage, whichever is greater, is exempt.

Nevada
Sec. 21-090

25% of disposable earnings for each week or an amount equal to 30 x the federal minimum hourly wage, whichever is greater.

New Hampshire
Sec. 512:21

Fifty times Federal minimum hourly wage on wages earned before the writ of garnishment is served; all wages earned after service of the writ.

New Jersey
Sec. 2A 17-56

10% of gross earnings or $142.50 per week minimum.

New Mexico
35-12-7

Either 75% of your weekly net earnings or 40 times the Federal minimum hourly wage, whichever is greater, is exempt.

New York
Sec. CPLR 5205:2

90% of debtor's income earned within 60 days of attempted garnishment is exempt.

North Carolina Sec. 1-362	Earned but unpaid wages received 60 days before writ is issued which are needed for support (as evidenced by affidavit or otherwise) are exempt.
North Dakota Sec. 32.09.1-03	Either 75% of your weekly net earnings or 40 times the Federal minimum hourly wage, whichever is greater, is exempt.
Ohio Sec. 2329.66(13)(a)	Either 75% of your weekly net earnings or 30 times the Federal minimum hourly wage, whichever is greater, is exempt.
Oklahoma Secs. 12-1171.1, 31-1	75% of wages earned within 90 days before writ is issued are exempt.
Oregon Sec. 23.185	An amount equal to 30 x the federal minimum hourly wage.
Pennsylvania Sec. 42-8127	Earned but unpaid wages (wages still in hands of employer) are exempt.
Rhode Island Secs. 9-26-4(6), 9-26-4(8)(A), 30-7-9	Wages due or accruing to any seaman are exempt wages, or salary paid from money appropriated for relief of poor or in aid of unemployment are exempt. Salary or wages due debtor, where debtor received relief from governmental agency within one year prior, are exempt. Wages or salary up to $50 are exempt. Salary of wife & minor children are exempt. Pay due or to become due to any member of the military for active service is exempt.
South Carolina	None.
South Dakota Sec. 15-20-12	Earned wages owed within 60 days before writ of garnishment is served which is needed for family support (as evidenced by affidavit or otherwise) are exempt.

Tennessee
Sec. 26-2-106,
26-2-107

Either 75% of your weekly net earnings or 30 times the Federal minimum hourly wage, whichever is greater, plus $2.50 per week per dependent child under 16, is exempt

Texas Property
Sec. 42.002(b)(1)

All earned but unpaid wages are exempt.

Utah
Sec. 70C-7-103(a)

Either 75% of your weekly net earnings or 30 times the Federal minimum hourly wage, whichever is greater, is exempt.

Vermont
Secs.3170, (b)(1), (b)(2)

Either 75% of your weekly net earnings or 30 times the Federal minimum hourly wage, whichever is greater, is exempt. All wages are exempt if you received welfare during 2 months before writ is issued.

Virginia
Sec. 34-19

Either 75% of your weekly net earnings or 30 times the Federal minimum hourly wage, whichever is greater, is exempt

Washington
Sec. 6.27.150

Either 75% of your weekly net earnings or 30 times the Federal minimum hourly wage, whichever is greater, is exempt.

West Virginia
Sec. 38-5A-3

Either 75% of your weekly net earnings or 30 times the Federal minimum hourly wage, whichever is greater, is exempt.

Wisconsin
Sec. 815.18

75% of income for each one-week pay period, but not less than 30 times the Federal minimum hourly wage per week, is exempt.

Wyoming
Sec. 1-15-511(a)

75% of your weekly net earnings or 30 times the Federal minimum hourly wage, whichever is greater, is exempt.

SAMPLE FLORIDA
DECLARATION OF DOMICILE

Board of County Commissioners - Broward County, Florida
Finance and Administrative Services Department
COUNTY RECORDS DIVISION

DECLARATION OF DOMICILE

This is my Declaration of Domicile in the State of Florida that I am filing this day in accordance and in conformity with Section 222.17, Florida Statutes.

I hereby declare that I became a bona fide resident of the State of Florida on:

_____(date of arrival)

I am, at the time of making this declaration, a bona fide resident of the State of Florida residing at:

_____ FLORIDA _____
(street and number)   (city)   (zip code)

which place of abode I recognize and intend to maintain as my permanent home, and if I maintain another place or places of abode in some other state or states, I hereby declare that my above-described residence and abode in the State of Florida constitutes my predominant and principal home, and I intend to continue it permanently as such.

I formerly resided at:

_____
(street and number)   (city)   (county)   (state)

and the place or places where I maintain another or other place or places of abode are as follows:

_____
(street and number)   (city)   (county)   (state)

_____
(street and number)   (city)   (county)   (state)

I understand that, as a legal resident of Florida: I am subject to intangible taxes; I must purchase Florida license plates for motor vehicles, if any, owned by me and/or my spouse; if I drive, I must have a Florida drivers license; if I vote, I must vote in the precinct of my legal domicile, and that my estate will be probated in Florida courts.

_____(Signature)   _____(Signature)
Print Name_____   Print Name_____

ID Produced_____   ID Produced_____
( ) United States Citizen   ( ) United States Citizen
( ) Citizen of _____   ( ) Citizen of _____
     Green Card #_____   Green Card #_____
     Date of Issuance_____   Date of Issuance_____

STATE OF FLORIDA
COUNTY OF BROWARD
Sworn to and subscribed before me *UNDER OATH* this _____ day of _____ , 20____.

_____
Signature of Notary Public, State of Florida

To be filed with the Department of Finance and Administrative Services - County Records Division
Penalty for perjury: up to five (5) years in state prison and $5000.00 fine: Chapter 837.012, F.S.

404-23 Rev. 02/15/01

214

PERSONAL ASSESSMENT AND PLANNING FOR THE FUTURE

17

DEBT AND ASSET EVALUATION

While taking care of your current financial problems you should also be thinking about the future. A job loss or long-term illness is rarely anticipated, but should be considered when making your decisions about how to handle your income and assets.

Tough economic times catch most people by surprise—they find they have to do whatever is necessary to get by, including getting family members to pitch in with income from part-time jobs. Saving for a rainy day is always recommended by financial planners—some are now even urging people to have a full year's living expenses available in the event of a major setback.

Saving a full year's living expenses is not easy when you are just trying to meet your monthly obligations. Making sure your property is safe or exempt from creditors is a step you can begin taking now. Before doing anything, however, make an honest assessment of where you are financially.

To help you better assess your financial situation, complete the chart on page 219. (If you decide to use consumer credit counseling services as mentioned in Chapter 3 under "Credit Counseling," you may be required to complete a similar personal financial assessment.)

First, you should determine exactly what your income and assets are, versus your liabilities. You may find that you have sufficient income and assets to satisfy your creditors, albeit at a reduced amount, for a period of time until you are again able to fully meet your obligations. (See the monthly expenses chart on page 220.)

Second, you should determine which of your assets have been given as security for a debt, such as your car, furniture, appliances and, of course, your home. These will be the assets subject to foreclosure or repossession by the creditor.(See the assets chart at the top of page 221.)

Third, you should determine which of your assets are currently subject to attachment or levy by a creditor. Perhaps you might consider selling some of these assets to pay down your debt, rather than having a creditor take them to satisfy a judgment.(See the collateral chart on the bottom of page 221.)

MAKING YOURSELF JUDGMENT-PROOF

Finally, you should consider methods by which you can make yourself judgment proof. Being *judgment proof* does not mean that a judgment cannot be entered against you—it simply means that anyone who has a judgment against you will be unable to collect it because any property you do own is exempt. As explained in previous chapters, certain property will be exempt from creditors, including judgment creditors and, in some cases, even the IRS.

If you have assets that you want to keep from potential creditors' hands, you may want to take more drastic measures. For instance, consider moving to a state with exemptions that would allow you to keep those assets.

Example: If you have a large amount of cash, you may want to move to a state with an unlimited homestead exemption and put your cash into your homestead.

Caution: If you are expecting a judgment to be entered against you in the near or immediate future, before transferring property in order to avoid the judgment creditor, contact an attorney. The transfer may be attacked by the creditor as a *fraudulent conveyance*. The same holds true if you are thinking about filing bankruptcy. A transfer can be set aside by the bankruptcy court as a preference. *Proper planning in these instances should include sound legal advice.*

In calculating the extent to which your property is exempt from creditors, be sure to determine whether the property is owned by you *and* your spouse jointly, and whether you live in a state where the joint property cannot be taken for the debt of only one spouse. (See "Your Assets" chart on page 221.)

The liens on your property include any loan made to you for which the property was taken as collateral (i.e. a mortgage or car loan), liens that attach to your property by law (such as contractor's liens), or liens that have resulted from judgments entered against you by a court.

The equity is the amount of money that would be left over when the property is sold and the loans against it (secured creditor) is paid. The equity, if not exempt from creditors, is the amount that would then be available to pay your other creditors.

Your financial health will be determined by comparing your monthly income with your monthly expenses, and by evaluating the amount of equity you have (if any) in your property. The exempt amounts are what would be left to you if your creditors obtained judgments and took your property as payment, or if you file for bankruptcy.

Below is an additional worksheet to help you in determining your equity in your property. Be honest with yourself when completing the form. Often, owners inflate the value of their property. Remember, what you paid for the property is not necessarily what it is worth, nor will you necessarily be able to sell it for as much as you paid.

If you have assets that are secured, (i.e. a mortgage against your house, or a loan against your car) you must remember that the creditor can take the property for payment of the debt. If the property is valuable, and little is owed on your loan, you should consider selling it yourself, paying the - creditor, and using the balance left to pay off other debts. (See the "Assets Given as Collateral" chart on page 221.)

If you have little or no equity in the property (the balance due on the loan equals or exceeds the value), consider selling it and asking the creditor to accept the buyer as the new borrower and releasing you from your obligations (unless the buyer can pay cash). Remember, if the creditor takes steps to repossess the property, any costs, including attorney's fees, may be added on the amount you already owe.

PERSONAL FINANCIAL ASSESSMENT

NET INCOME (AFTER TAXES):

Source	Monthly Amt	Non-IRS Exempt? (Y or N)	IRS Exempt? (Y or N)	If Exempt How Much?
Wages				
Social Security				
Pension Fund				
Alimony/Support				
Public Assistance				
Disability				
Other (type)				
TOTALS				*

*The total of the exempt amounts is the amount of income you will be able to keep every month regardless of any judgment collection efforts or garnishments by creditors. If the IRS is among your creditors, make sure you use the third column to determine your exemptions.

MONTHLY EXPENSES

	Amount
Mortgage/Rent	
Home maintenance	
Homeowners insurance	
Food	
Food away from home	
Gas/Electric	
Water	
Trash collection	
Phone	
Car payment(s)	
Gas/oil/maintenance	
Car insurance	
Other transportation	
Life insurance	
Health insurance	
School/Books/Tuition	
Child care	
Child support/Alimony	
Medical expenses	
Clothing	
Subscriptions	
Cable TV	
Dues/Church tithes	
Other	
TOTAL:	$

(Your total monthly expenses, deducted from your total net monthly income listed on page 219, should give you an indication of your financial situation. You may be able to reduce or eliminate some of these expenses in order to pay other debts.)

YOUR ASSETS

	Value	Equity	$ Amt. of Liens on Property	Non-IRS Exempt? (Y or N)	IRS Exempt? (Y or N)
Homestead					
Other Real Estate					
Automobiles					
Household Goods (Furniture, Appliances)					
Trade Tools					
Other (examples: stocks, bonds, CD's, savings)					
TOTALS					

ASSETS GIVEN AS COLLATERAL

Name of Asset	Value	Creditor	Balance of Secured Debt	Equity
House/Real Estate	$		$	$
Other Real Estate	$		$	$
Automobile	$		$	$
Automobile	$		$	$
Furniture	$		$	$
Stereo/Television	$		$	$
Jewelry	$		$	$
Other	$		$	$
Other	$		$	$

GLOSSARY

A

acceleration. To speed up; to bring future obligations current.

adjudication. The act of a court of law making an order or judgment.

affidavit. A sworn, written declaration, usually signed before a notary public.

assignment (of wages or other property). To transfer an interest in certain property to another.

audit. An official examination of accounts and records.

B

beneficiary. Person designated to receive funds or other property from an estate or trust.

bond. A written promise of another (surety) to pay a debt in the event the debtor fails to pay.

C

civil remedies. The legal means of enforcing a civil (as opposed to criminal) right.

collateral. Security (usually property) pledged for the payment of a loan.

collection agency. A business which collects outstanding bills for other businesses and individuals, typically in exchange for a percentage of the amount collected.

complaint. Also called a **petition**, the first document filed in a civil lawsuit.

compliance. Acting in accordance with certain legal requirements.

consolidation. Act of combining two or more debts into one.

consumer. Usually an individual who purchases and/or uses goods and services.

consumer lease. A lease or rental agreement, typically for a vehicle or household goods, between a business and an individual.

contingent liability. A liability which does not become effective until another acts or fails to act in accordance with an agreement.

counterclaim. A claim filed by an individual against whom a first claim has already been filed by another individual or business.

creditor. An individual or business to whom one owes a debt.

credit report. A summary of credit information on a individual which is prepared by a credit reporting agency.

credit reporting agency. A business which assembles and evaluates consumer credit information for the purpose of providing credit reports to third parties.

D

damages. The estimate money equivalent of an injury or wrong.

deadbeat list. List of those who owe money but have failed to pay.

deed of trust. Similar to a mortgage, title to property held by a trustee until a debt affecting real property is paid in full.

default. Failure to meet an obligation, such as a loan payment or court appearance.

deferment. Postponement, particularly of collecting a debt.

deficiency/notice of deficiency. The amount by which a creditor's claim is not satisfied, and the notice thereof to the debtor.

deposition. Statement taken under oath which is to be used in court proceedings.

disclosure/disclose. The act of revealing certain information, particularly to a debtor regarding his loan.

E

economic hardship. Financially severely difficult.

equitable title. The right of ownership, although legal title is held by another.

equity. The amount of value of property remaining after deducting the mortgage and other pledges or liens rightfully against the property.

equity line. A line of credit, or loan, given by a lender with the equity in real estate given as collateral.

execute/execution. To carry out the terms of a legal document, esp. a judgment.

F

fair market value. Price at which a willing buyer and willing seller will trade.

file segregation. Establishment of a new credit identity with inaccurate information.

financial statement. A statement, usually requested by a lender, which describes your property, its value, your income and liabilities (debt), indicating your actual financial condition.

forbearance. Refrain from doing something (i.e. collecting a debt).

foreclose/foreclosure. The termination of all of the rights of the borrower in property given as collateral to the mortgagee or lender.

G

good faith. With good intentions; (i.e. with most accurate information available).

governmental instrumentality. An agency of the government.

guarantor. One who guarantors the debt or obligation of another.

guaranty. A pledge or promise given as security for payment of a debt or obligation.

I

indemnification. Act of agreeing to compensate someone for any loss or damage.

J

joint and several liability. Referring to financial obligations, all signers are jointly as well as individually liable for the debt.

judgment. A court decision.

judgment proof. Immune from results of a judgment (i.e. having no assets from which a creditor can collect a money judgment).

junior interest. An interest (typically in property) which is inferior to another's interest.

L

lender. An individual or business (typically a bank or financing company) who loans money to another.

lien. A claim against property for the payment of a debt or obligation.

M

mortgage. The pledge of property as security for a loan, usually real property.

N

negligence/negligent. To omit doing something through indifference or carelessness.

O

obligor. One who is obligated to act (i.e. one who owes money).

open-end credit. A sum of money made available to an individual against which amounts can be drawn repeatedly and at various interest rates, such as a credit card or equity-line mortgage.

P

periodic rates. Interest rates which change from time to time as specified in the loan documents.

personal property. Also referred to a *chattel,* any property which is moveable as opposed to real estate or fixed to real estate.

petition. *See* **complaint.**

principal. The amount of money borrowed (as opposed to interest).

pro rata. In proportion to something; according to a certain rate.

public record. Records which are kept by a governmental body and available to the public for review.

punitive damages. Compensation awarded for an injury or wrong which are intended to punish the one who committed such injury or wrong.

purchase money mortgage. Mortgage given by the buyer back to the seller of property.

Q

quitclaim deed. Transfer of title to real estate which does not contain any guaranties or warranties.

R

real property. Real estate, land.

Regulation Z. Federal Truth-in-Lending regulations found in the Code of Federal Regulations, Banks and Banking section.

remedies. The means of enforcing a right.

repossess. To regain possession of something; also used when the creditor is taking possession of collateral after default in the payments by the debtor.

rescission. Withdrawal or cancellation.

residential mortgage transaction. Transaction with the lender whereby real property is given as collateral in exchange for funds.

residual value. The value of property at the end of a specific time period, esp. at the end of a lease term.

right of set-off. Typically a lender's right to take money from a borrower's other accounts to pay for a specific debt owed that lender.

S

secured. Protected (pledge of property to assure a creditor of payment).

security interest. An interest in property given as collateral for a debt.

separate property. An individual's property which is not co-mingled with another's property.

statutes. A written law which is passed by a governing authority, usually a state legislature or Congress.

statute of limitations. A statute stating the period of time in which a claim can be brought before a court.

superior claim. A claim against property, usually by a lender, which takes priority over another claim, i.e. which must be paid before another claim against the same property can be paid.

T

tenants by the entireties. A manner of holding title to property by husband and wife, recognized in nearly one-third of all states, whereby each party holds title to the entire property, and it cannot be divided without the consent of both husband and wife.

U

underwriting. To assume liability for something to the extent of a certain dollar amount.

unsecured. Unprotected; without security.

V

void/voidable. Without legal force or effect/to cause to be without legal force or effect.

W

willfully. Intentionally.

writ. A legal document, ordering an authorized person to do a certain act (or to refrain from doing something).

APPENDIX A
U.S. GOVERNMENT PRINTING OFFICES

Information about your rights under the Consumer Credit Protection Act, including Truth-in-Lending and Regulation Z, should be available at the U.S. Government bookstores listed in this appendix.

Alabama
U.S. Government Bookstore
O'Neill Building
2021 Third Ave. North
Birmingham, AL 35203
205-731-1056
Fax: 205-731-3444

California
U.S. Government Bookstore
ARCO Plaza, C-Level
505 South Flower Street
Los Angeles, CA 90071
213-239-9844
Fax: 213-239-9848

U.S. Government Bookstore
450 Golden Gate Ave.
Box 36104
San Francisco, CA 94102
415-355-4930

Colorado
U.S. Government Bookstore
1660 WynKoop
Suite 130
Denver, CO 80202
303-844-3964
Fax: 303-844-4000

U.S. Government Bookstore
Norwest Banks Building
201 West 8th Street
Pueblo, CO 81003
719-544-3142
Fax: 719-544-6719

District of Columbia
U.S. Government Bookstore
U.S. Government Printing Office
710 Capitol Street, NW
Washington, DC 20401
202-512-0132
Fax: 202-512-1355

U.S. Government Bookstore
1510 H. Street, NW
Washington, DC 20005
202-653-5075
Fax: 202-376-5055

Florida
U.S. Government Bookstore
100 West Bay Street
Suite 100
Jacksonville, FL 32202
904-353-0569
Fax: 904-353-1280

Georgia
U.S. Government Bookstore
First Union Plaza
999 Peachtree St, NE
Atlanta, GA 30309-3964
404-347-1900
Fax: 404-347-1897

Illinois
U.S. Government Bookstore
One Congress Center
401 South State St., Suite 124
Chicago, IL 60605
312-353-5133
Fax: 312-353-1590

Maryland
Government Bookstore
U.S. Government Printing Office
Warehouse Sales Outlet
8660 Cherry Lane
Laurel, MD 20707
301-953-7974
301-792-0262
Fax: 301-498-8995

Massachusetts
U.S. Government Bookstore
Thomas P. O'Neill Building
Room 169
10 Causeway Street
Boston, MA 02222
617-720-4180
Fax: 617-720-5753

Michigan
U.S. Government Bookstore
Suite 160, Federal Bldg.
477 Michigan Ave
Detroit, MI 48226
313-226-7816
313-226-4698

Missouri
U.S. Government Bookstore
120 Bannister Mall
5600 East Bannister Road
Kansas City, MO 64137
816-765-2256
Fax: 816-767-8233

New York
U.S. Government Bookstore
Rm. 110, Federal Building
26 Federal Plaza
New York, NY 10278
212-264-3825
Fax: 212-264-9318

Ohio
U.S. Government Bookstore
Room 1653, Federal Building
1240 E. 9th Street
Cleveland, OH 44199
714-469-6956
Fax: 216-522-4714

U.S. Government Bookstore
Room 207, Federal Building
200 N. High Street
Columbus, OH 43215
614-469-6953
Fax: 614-469-5374

Oregon
U.S. Government Bookstore
1305 SW First Avenue
Portland, OR 97201-5801
503-221-6217
Fax: 503-225-0563

Pennsylvania
U.S. Government Bookstore
Robert Morris Building
100 North 17th Street
Philadelphia, PA 19103
412-495-5021
412-395-4547

U.S. Government Bookstore
Rm 118, Federal Building
1000 Liberty Avenue
Pittsburgh, PA 15222
412-644-2721
Fax: 412-644-4547

Texas
U.S. Government Bookstore
Rm 1C50, Federal Bldg
1100 Commerce St
Dallas, TX 75242
214-767-0076
Fax: 214-767-3239

U.S. Government Bookstore
Texas Crude Building
801 Travis Street, Suite 120
Houston, TX 77002
713-228-1187
Fax: 713-228-1186

Washington
U.S. Government Bookstore
Rm 194, Federal Building
915 Second Avenue
Seattle, WA 98174
206-553-4270
Fax: 206-553-6717

Wisconsin
U.S. Government Bookstore
Suite 150, Reuss Federal Plaza
310 W. Wisconsin Avenue
Milwaukee, WI 53203
414-297-1304
Fax: 414-297-1300

> ***Note.*** Mail orders can also be sent to:
> Superintendent of Documents
> Washington, DC 20402

APPENDIX B
STATE-BY-STATE
CONSUMER AFFAIRS
OFFICES

A more comprehensive list, including web addresses, can be found at:

http://www.pueblo.gsa.gov/crh/state.htm

Alabama
Consumer Protection Division
Office of Attorney General
11 South Union Street
Montgomery, AL 36130
800-392-5658; 334-242-7335
http://www.ago.state.al.us

Alaska
Office of the Attorney General
1031 W. 4th Ave.
Suite 200
Anchorage, AK 99501
907-465-3600
http://www.law.state.ak.us/con-
sumer/
complaint.form

Arizona
Consumer Complaints
Office of the Attorney General
1275 W. Washington Street
Phoenix, AZ 85007
800-532-8431; 602-542-5763
http://www.ag.state.az.us/
consumer/index.html

Arkansas
Attorney General's Office
Consumer Protection
200 Tower Building
323 Center Street
Little Rock, AR 72201
800-482-8982; 501-602-2007
http://www.ag.state.ar.us/

California
Office of Attorney General
P.O. Box 944255
Sacramento, CA 94244
916-445-9555
http://www.caag.state.ca.us/

Colorado
Consumer Protection Unit
Office of Attorney General
1525 Sherman St., 7th Floor
Denver, CO 80203
303-866-5189
800-222-4444
http://www.ago.state.co.us

Connecticut

Dept. of Consumer Protection
165 Capitol Avenue
Hartford, CT 06106
860-713-6300
http://www.cslib.org/attygenl/

Delaware

Division of Consumer Affairs
820 North French Street
Wilmington, DE 19801
302-577-8600
http://www.state.de.us/attygen/

District of Columbia

Department of Consumer &
  Regulatory Affairs
614 H. Street, N.W., Room 16
Washington, D.C. 20001
202-727-7000

Florida

Division of Consumer Services
Department of Agriculture &
  Consumer Services
218 Mayo Building
Tallahassee, FL 32399
800-435-7352; 904-488-2226
http://www.fl-ag.com

Georgia

Office of Consumer Affairs
2 Martin Luther King Jr. Drive
Suite 356
Plaza Level East
Atlanta, GA 30334
404-651-2000; 404-651-9018
http://www2.state.ga.us/gaoca

Hawaii

Office of Consumer Protection
Department of Commerce &

Consumer Affairs
345 Kekuanaonoa St.
Room 12
Hilo, HI 96720
808-933-0910
http://www.state.hi.us/dcca/

Idaho

Consumer Protection Unit
Office of Attorney General
Statehouse Room 113A
P.O. Box 83720
Boise, ID 83720-0010
800-432-3545; 208-334-2424
http://www.state.id.us/ag/
consumer/consumer.htm

Illinois

Office of Attorney General
Consumer Protection
1001 E. Main Street
Carbondale, IL 62901
618-529-6400
http://www.ag.state.il.us

Indiana

Consumer Protection Division
Office of Attorney General
219 State House
Indianapolis, IN 46204
800-382-5516; 317-232-6330
http://www.ai.org/hoosieradvocate

Iowa

Consumer Protection Division
Office of Attorney General
1305 East Walnut
Des Moines, IA 50319
515-281-5926
http://www.state.ia.us/
government/ag/consumer.html

Kansas
Office of Attorney General
Consumer Protection Division
120 SW 10th Street
Topeka, KS 66612-1597
800-432-2310; 785-296-3751
http://www.ink.org/public.ksag

Kentucky
Consumer Protection Division
Office of Attorney General
1024 Capital Center Drive
Frankfort, KY 40601
800-432-9257; 502-696-5389
http://www.law.state.ky.us/cp

Louisiana
Attn: Consumer Protection
    Division
301 Main Street, Suite 1250
Baton Rouge, LA 70801
225-342-9639
http://www.laag.com

Maine
Attorney General Consumer
    Mediation Service
State House Station No. 6
Augusta, ME 04333-0035
207-626-8800
http://www.state.me.us/ag

Maryland
Consumer Protection Division
200 St. Paul Place, 16th Floor
Baltimore, Maryland 21202
410-528-8662
http://www.oag.state.md.us/
consumer

Massachusetts
Executive Office of Consumer
    Affairs
One Ashburton Place, Room 1411

Boston, MA 02108
617-727-7780
http://www.ago.state.ma.us/
internet.asp

Michigan
Consumers Protection Division
Office of Attorney General
P.O. Box 30212
Lansing, MI 48909
517-373-1140
http://www.ci.detroit.mi.us

Minnesota
Consumer Affairs Division
Office of Attorney General
1400 St. Capital
445 Minnesota Street
St. Paul, MN 55101
800-657-3787; 612-296-3353
http://www.ag.state.mn.us/
consumer

Mississippi
Consumer Protection Division
Office of Attorney General
P.O. Box 22947
Jackson, MS 39225
601-359-4230
http://www.ago.state.ms.us/
consprot.htm

Missouri
Public Protection
Office of Attorney General
P.O. Box 899
Jefferson City, MO 65102
800-392-8222; 573-751-6887
http://www.ago.state.mo.us

Montana

Office of Consumer Affairs
Department of Commerce
1424 9th Avenue
Helena, MT 59620
406-444-4312

Nebraska

Office of Attorney General
Consumer Protection Division
2115 State Capitol
Lincoln, NE 68509
402-471-2682
http://www.nol.org

Nevada

Consumer Affairs Division
Department of Consumer Affairs
State Mail Room Complex
1850 E. Sahara, Suite 101
Las Vegas, NV 89104
702-486-7355
http://www.fyiconsumer.org

New Hampshire

Consumer Protection and
  Antitrust Division
Office of Attorney General
State House Annex
Concord, NH 03301
603-271-3641
http://www.state.nh.us/nhdoj/
consumercpb.html

New Jersey

Office of Consumer Protection
P.O. Box 45025
Newark, NJ 07101
973-504-6200
http://www.state.nj.us/lps/ca/
home.htm

New Mexico

Consumer Protection Division
Office of Attorney General
P.O. Drawer 1508
Santa Fe, NM 87504-1508
505-827-6060
http://www.ago.state.nm.us

New York

State Consumer Protection Board
State Capitol
Albany, NY 12224
518-474-5481
http://www.org.state.ny.us

North Carolina

Consumer Protection Section
Department of Justice
P.O. Box 629
Raleigh, NC 27602
919-716-6000
http://www.jus.state.nc.us/
cpframe.htm

North Dakota

Consumer Protection
Office of Attorney General
600 East Boulevard, Dept. 125
Bismark, ND 58505
800-472-2600; 701-328-3404
http://www.ag.state.nd.us/ndag/
cpat/cpat.html

Ohio

Consumer Protection Division
Office of Attorney General
30 East Broad Street, 25th Floor
Columbus, OH 43215-3428
800-282-0515; 614-466-8831
http://www.oh.us

Oklahoma

Consumer Protection Division
Office of Attorney General
4545 N. Lincoln Blvd. #104
Oklahoma City, OK 73105
405-521-3653
http://www.oag.state.ok.us

Oregon

Financial Fraud Section
Department of Justice
Justice Building
Salem, OR 97310
503-378-4320
http://www.doj.state.or.us

Pennsylvania

Bureau of Consumer Protection
Office of Attorney General
132 Kline Village
14th Floor Strawberry Square
Harrisburg, PA 17120
800-441-2555; 717-787-9707
http://www.attorneygeneral.gov

Rhode Island

Consumer Protection Division
Office of Attorney General
150 South Main Street
Providence, RI 02903
401-274-4400
http://www.creditcounseling.org

South Carolina

Department of Consumer Affairs
P.O. Box 5757
Columbia, SC 29250
800-922-1594; 803-734-9452
http://www.state.sc.us/consumer

South Dakota

Division of Consumer Affairs
Office of Attorney General
State Capital Building
500 E. Capitol Avenue
Pierre, SD 57501
(605) 773-4400

Tennessee

State of Tennessee
Department of Commerce and
Insurance
Division of Consumer Affairs
500 James Robertson Parkway,
5th Floor
Nashville, Tn 37243-0600
800-342-8385; 615-741-4737
http://www.state.tn.us/consumer

Texas

Consumer Protection Division
Office of Attorney General
P.O. Box 12548
Austin, TX 78711
512-463-2185
http://www.aog.state.tx.us

Utah

Division of Consumer Protection
Department of Business
  Regulation
160 East 300 South
P.O. Box 146704
Salt Lake City, UT 84145-6704
801-530-6601
http://www.commerce.state.ut.us

Vermont

Consumer Assistance Program
Office of Attorney General
104 Morrill Hall
Burlington, VT 05405
800-649-2424; 802-656-3183
http://www.state.vt.us/atg

Virginia

Division of Consumer Affairs
Box 1163
Richmond, VA 23219
800-552-9963; 804-786-2042
http://www.vdacs.state.va.us

Washington

Consumer Protection Division
Office of Attorney General
900 4th Avenue Room 2000
Seattle, WA 98164
800-551-4636; 206-464-6684
http://www.wa.gov/ago

West Virginia

Consumer Protection Division
Office of Attorney General
812 Quarrier Street, 6th Floor
P.O. Box 1789
Charleston, WV 25326-1789
800-368-8808; 304-558-8986

Wisconsin

Division of Trade and Consumer
  Protection
Department of Agriculture, Trade
  and Consumer Protection
P.O. Box 8911
Madison, WI 53708
608-224-4853
http://www.datcp.state.wi.us

Wyoming

Consumer Affairs Division
Office of Attorney General
123 State Capitol Building
Cheyenne, WY 82002
307-777-7874
http://www.state.wy.us/~ag/
consumer.htm

APPENDIX C
FEDERAL TRADE COMMISSION REGIONAL OFFICES

States in Region	Office and Addresses
Alabama, Florida, Georgia Mississippi, North Carolina South Carolina, Tennessee, Virginia	Rm. 1000, 1718 Peachtree St. NW Atlanta, Georgia 30367 404-656-1399
Connecticut, Maine, Massachusetts, New Hampshire, Rhode Island, Vermont	Room 1184, 10 Causeway Street Boston, Massachusetts 02222-1073 617-424-5960
Illinois, Indiana, Iowa, Kentucky Minnesota, Missouri, Wisconsin	Suite 1437, 55 E. Monroe Street Chicago, Illinois 60603 312-353-4423
Michigan, Ohio, Pennsylvania West Virginia, Delaware, Maryland	Suite 520-A, 668 Euclid Avenue Cleveland, Ohio 44114 216-522-4207
Arkansas, Louisiana, New Mexico Oklahoma, Texas	Suite 500 100 N. Central Expressway Dallas, Texas 75201
Colorado, Kansas, Montana, Nebraska, North Dakota, South Dakota, Utah, Wyoming	Suite 2900, 1405 Curtis Street Denver, Colorado 80202-2393 303-844-2271

STATES IN REGION	OFFICE AND ADDRESSES
Arizona, Southern California	Suite 13209, 11000 Wilshire Blvd. Los Angeles, California 90024 310-235-4000
Northern California, Hawaii, Nevada	Suite 570, 901 Market Street San Francisco, California 94103 415-356-5270
Alaska, Idaho, Oregon, Washington	Room 2806, 915 2nd Avenue Seattle, Washington 98174 206-220-6363
New York, New Jersey	13th Floor, 150 William Street New York, New York 10038 212-264-1207

APPENDIX D
STATUTES OF
LIMITATION

The *Statute of Limitations* is the law that sets the time period in which a lawsuit can be filed after a specified event. The time periods listed on the following pages are all in years. More detailed information follows the listing.

A *written contract* is one that has been signed by the parties. A *promissory note* is a document that has been signed stating the amount to be paid and the manner in which it is to be paid. The promissory note usually includes a provision for default—i.e. what the creditor or lender can do in the event payment is not made as required in the note.

As you will see below, the time period in which a creditor can file a lawsuit to collect on a promissory note is generally the same as the time limitation for suing on a written contract. Only two states, Delaware and Louisiana, set a different time limitation for suing on a promissory note.

An *oral contract* is just that—a verbal agreement to do something that has not been reduced to writing and signed by the parties.

The list is by no means exhaustive. You should consult your state laws for more specific information. Typically, the reference to the Statute of Limitations can be found in the index to your state statutes, under the heading "Limitation of Actions." To get you started, below is a list of some of the statutory references, state by state. However, these include only the limitations listed above.

There may be additional and different time limitations for lawsuits on sales contracts, open-end revolving accounts, lawsuits for damages, etc. Also, you will be able to find your state's time limitation for filing a lawsuit to collect a judgment.

NOTE: *All time periods listed refer to years.*

State	Written Contracts	Promissory Notes	Oral Contracts	Statutory Reference
Alabama	6	6	6	6-23-33, 6-2-34
Alaska	6	6	6	09.10.050, 45-02-725
Arizona	6	5	3	12-548, 12-543
Arkansas	5	6	3	16-56-115, 16-56-105
California	4	4	2	CCP 337
Colorado	6	6	6	13-80-103.5
Connecticut	6	6	3	52-576, 52-581
Delaware	3	6	3	10-8106, 10-8109
District of Col.	3	3	3	12-301
Florida	5	5	4	95.11
Georgia	6	6	4	9-3-24, 9-3-25
Hawaii	6	6	6	657-1
Idaho	5	10	4	5-216, 5-217
Illinois	10	6	5	13-206, 13-205
Indiana	10	10	6	34-1-2-1
Iowa	10	10	5	614.1
Kansas	5	5	3	60.511, 60.512
Kentucky	15	15	5	413.090, 413.120
Louisiana	10	10	10	CC 3509, 3478
Maine	6	6	6	14-751

State	Written Contracts	Promissory Notes	Oral Contracts	Statutory Reference
Maryland	3	6	3	CJ 5-101
Massachusetts	6	6	6	260.2
Michigan	6	6	6	600.5813, 451.435
Minnesota	6	6	6	541.05
Mississippi	3	3	3	752-725, 15-1-29
Missouri	10	10	5	516.110, 516.120
Montana	8	8	5	27-2-202
Nebraska	5	6	4	25-205, 25-206
Nevada	6	3	4	11.90
New Hampshire	3	6	3	508:4
New Jersey	6	6	6	2A:14-1
New Mexico	6	6	4	37-1-3, 37-1-4
New York	6	6	6	CPLR 213(2)
North Carolina	3	5	3	CP 1-52.
North Dakota	6	6	6	28-01-16
Ohio	15	15	6	2305.06, 2305.07
Oklahoma	5	5	3	12 Sec. 95
Oregon	6	6	6	12.080
Pennsylvania	6	4	4	42 Sec. 5525
Rhode Island	15	10	15	9-1-13(a)
South Carolina	10	3	10	15-3-350
South Dakota	6	6	6	15-2-13
Tennessee	6	6	6	28-3-109
Texas	4	4	4	16.004
Utah	6	6	4	28-12-23, 28-12-25
Vermont	6	5	6	12-511
Virginia	5	6	3	8.01-246
Washington	6	6	3	4.16.040, 4.16.080
West Virginia	10	6	5	55-2-6
Wisconsin	6	10	6	893.43
Wyoming	10	10	8	1-3-105

APPENDIX E
FREQUENTLY REFERENCED
LAWS

Consumer Credit Act, U.S.C., Title 15, Chapter 41 covers disclosure requirements for most credit transactions, credit reporting agencies, and collection agencies. The Act now includes the following laws which are referenced in this book:

- Consumer Credit Cost Disclosure (Truth in Lending), U.S.C., Title 15, Chapter 41, Section 1601 and the Truth-in-Lending regulations (Regulation Z), Code of Federal Regulations Title 12, Part 226, ensuring that everyone who has a need for consumer credit is given meaningful information regarding the cost of the credit.

United States Code, Title 15, Chapter 41 includes the following:

- Fair Credit Billing Act (regulating the manner in which you are billed by creditors and the information which must be disclosed to you).
- Consumer Leasing Act of 1976.
- Credit advertising.

(See Truth in Lending Regulations Appendices for sample calculations and disclosure form.)

- Restrictions on Garnishment are set forth in U.S.C., Title 15, Section 1667, Title III.

- Fair Debt Collection Practices Act, U.S.C., Title 15, Section 1692, Public Law 95-109 (regulating the practices of collection agencies).

- Consumer Credit Reporting Act of 1996, U.S.C., Title 15, Section 1601, Public Law 104-208 (regulating the practices of credit reporting agencies or credit bureaus).

- U.S.C., Title 11, U.S. Bankruptcy Code generally.

- U.S.C., Title 11, Chapter 7, Liquidation.

- U.S.C., Title 11, Chapter 13, Adjustment of Debts of an Individual with Regular Income (Wage Earner Plan).

- U.S.C., Title 29, Internal Revenue Code generally.

- U.S.C., Title 29, Section 6334 - Internal Revenue Exemptions.

INDEX

regulation Z, 88, 92-95, 97, 102,
103, 138, 139
rent, 11, 36
repossession, 22, 145-152, 216, 219
rescission, 98-100
residual value calculation, 120-121
Revised Uniform Reciprocal
Enforcement of Support Act, 32
right of set-off, 21

S

Sallie Mae, 27-28, 31
secured debt. *See* debt
Securities and Exchange
Commission, 101
security interest. *See* debt
seller-financing, 13
service of process, 127-129
social security, 17, 188
social security number, 62
Soldiers' and Sailors' Civil Relief
Act, 136, 140, 150
sole proprietorship, 24
spouse, 5, 23, 33, 34, 156, 182, 192,
193, 194, 197-198, 200, 217
statute, 33, 154, 162, 179
statute of limitations, 60, 70, 157
stockholder, 24
stocks, 20, 21, 187
student loan. *See* loans
subpoena, 47
summons, 155-156, 158

T

tax identification number, 62
taxes, 17, 26-27, 28, 34, 60, 66,
75-86, 118, 173, 183, 185, 186,
197, 208
deductions, 80
examiner, 81, 82
income, 28, 34, 183, 186, 197
levy, 79
payroll, 26, 27
returns, 80, 82, 197

taxpayer assistance order, 78
taxpayers bill of rights, 78
TransUnion. *See* credit bureau
trustee, 184
truth in lending, 87-108
disclosures, 88, 90, 93, 96-97,
101
Truth in Lending Act, 117

U

UIFSA. *See* Uniform Interstate
Family Support Act
unconscionability, 157
unemployment, 30, 79, 199
Uniform Enforcement of Foreign
Judgments Act, 159
Uniform Interstate Family Support
Act, 32
unsecured debt. *See* debt
URESA. *See* Revised Uniform
Reciprocal Enforcement of
Support Act
utilities, 36

W

wage assignment, 37
wage earners plan, 16
wage garnishment, 12, 13, 171-
175, 208
exemptions, 173
wages, 33, 170, 199, 208
warranties, 119, 157
implied, 157
welfare, 65
Welfare Reform Act, 32
witness, 51
workman's compensation, 79
writ of attachment, 178
writ of execution, 176

SPHINX® PUBLISHING ORDER FORM

TO:	SHIP TO:

e #	Terms	F.O.B.	Chicago, IL	Ship Date

Charge my: ☐ VISA ☐ MasterCard ☐ American Express ☐ **Money Order or Personal Check**

Credit Card Number

Expiration Date

y	ISBN	Title	Retail
	SPHINX PUBLISHING NATIONAL TITLES		
___	1-57248-148-X Cómo Hacer su Propio Testamento	$16.95
___	1-57248-147-1 Cómo Solicitar su Propio Divorcio	$24.95
___	1-57248-160-9 Essential Guide to Real Estate Leases	$18.95
___	1-57248-139-0 Grandparents' Rights (3E)	$24.95
___	1-57248-087-4 Guía de Inmigración a Estados Unidos (2E)	$24.95
___	1-57248-103-X Help Your Lawyer Win Your Case (2E)	$14.95
___	1-57071-164-X How to Buy a Condominium or Townhome	$19.95
___	1-57071-223-9 How to File Your Own Bankruptcy (4E)	$21.95
___	1-57248-132-3 How to File Your Own Divorce (4E)	$24.95
___	1-57248-100-5 How to Form a DE Corporation from Any State	$24.95
___	1-57248-083-1 How to Form a Limited Liability Company	$22.95
___	1-57248-099-8 How to Form a Nonprofit Corporation	$24.95
___	1-57248-133-1 How to Form Your Own Corporation (3E)	$24.95
___	1-57071-343-X How to Form Your Own Partnership	$22.95
___	1-57248-119-6 How to Make Your Own Will (2E)	$16.95
___	1-57071-331-6 How to Negotiate Real Estate Contracts (3E)	$18.95
___	1-57248-124-2 How to Register Your Own Copyright (3E)	$21.95
___	1-57248-104-8 How to Register Your Own Trademark (3E)	$21.95
___	1-57071-349-9 How to Win Your Unemployment Compensation Claim	$21.95
___	1-57248-118-8 How to Write Your Own Living Will (2E)	$16.95
___	1-57071-344-8 How to Write Your Own Premarital Agreement (2E)	$21.95
___	1-57248-158-7 Incorporate in Nevada from Any State	$24.95
___	1-57071-333-2 Jurors' Rights (2E)	$12.95
___	1-57071-400-2 Legal Research Made Easy (2E)	$16.95
___	1-57071-336-7 Living Trusts and Simple Ways to Avoid Probate (2E)	$22.95
___	1-57071-345-6 Most Valuable Bus. Legal Forms You'll Ever Need (2E)	$19.95
___	1-57071-346-4 Most Valuable Corporate Forms You'll Ever Need (2E)	$24.95

Qty	ISBN	Title	Retail
___	1-57248-130-7 Most Valuable Personal Legal Forms You'll Ever Need	$24.95
___	1-57248-098-X The Nanny and Domestic Help Legal Kit	$22.95
___	1-57248-089-0 Neighbor v. Neighbor (2E)	$16.95
___	1-57071-348-0 The Power of Attorney Handbook (3E)	$19.95
___	1-57248-149-8 Repair Your Own Credit and Deal with Debt	$18.95
___	1-57071-337-5 Social Security Benefits Handbook (2E)	$16.95
___	1-57071-399-5 Unmarried Parents' Rights	$19.95
___	1-57071-354-5 U.S.A. Immigration Guide (3E)	$19.95
___	1-57248-138-2 Winning Your Personal Injury Claim (2E)	$24.95
___	1-57248-097-1 Your Right to Child Custody, Visitation and Support	$22.95
___	1-57248-157-9 Your Rights When You Owe Too Much	$16.95
	CALIFORNIA TITLES		
___	1-57248-150-1 CA Power of Attorney Handbook (2E)	$18.95
___	1-57248-151-X How to File for Divorce in CA (3E)	$26.95
___	1-57071-356-1 How to Make a CA Will	$16.95
___	1-57248-145-5 How to Probate and Settle an Estate in California	$26.95
___	1-57248-146-3 How to Start a Business in CA	$18.95
___	1-57071-358-8 How to Win in Small Claims Court in CA	$16.95
___	1-57071-359-6 Landlords' Rights and Duties in CA	$21.95
	FLORIDA TITLES		
___	1-57071-363-4 Florida Power of Attorney Handbook (2E)	$16.95
___	1-57248-093-9 How to File for Divorce in FL (6E)	$24.95
___	1-57071-380-4 How to Form a Corporation in FL (4E)	$24.95
___	1-57248-086-6 How to Form a Limited Liability Co. in FL	$22.95
___	1-57071-401-0 How to Form a Partnership in FL	$22.95
___	1-57248-113-7 How to Make a FL Will (6E)	$16.95

Form Continued   *Subtotal* _____

Qty	ISBN	Title	Retail
		FLORIDA TITLES (CONT'D)	
_____	1-57248-088-2	How to Modify Your FL Divorce Judgment (4E)	$24.95
_____	1-57248-144-7	How to Probate and Settle and Estate in FL (4E)	$26.95
_____	1-57248-081-5	How to Start a Business in FL (5E)	$16.95
_____	1-57071-362-6	How to Win in Small Claims Court in FL (6E)	$16.95
_____	1-57248-123-4	Landlords' Rights and Duties in FL (8E)	$21.95
		GEORGIA TITLES	
_____	1-57248-137-4	How to File for Divorce in GA (4E)	$21.95
_____	1-57248-075-0	How to Make a GA Will (3E)	$16.95
_____	1-57248-140-4	How to Start a Business in Georgia (2E)	$16.95
		ILLINOIS TITLES	
_____	1-57071-405-3	How to File for Divorce in IL (2E)	$21.95
_____	1-57071-415-0	How to Make an IL Will (2E)	$16.95
_____	1-57071-416-9	How to Start a Business in IL (2E)	$18.95
_____	1-57248-078-5	Landlords' Rights & Duties in IL	$21.95
		MASSACHUSETTS TITLES	
_____	1-57248-128-5	How to File for Divorce in MA (3E)	$24.95
_____	1-57248-115-3	How to Form a Corporation in MA	$24.95
_____	1-57248-108-0	How to Make a MA Will (2E)	$16.95
_____	1-57248-106-4	How to Start a Business in MA (2E)	$18.95
_____	1-57248-107-2	Landlords' Rights and Duties in MA (2E)	$21.95
		MICHIGAN TITLES	
_____	1-57071-409-6	How to File for Divorce in MI (2E)	$21.95
_____	1-57248-077-7	How to Make a MI Will (2E)	$16.95
_____	1-57071-407-X	How to Start a Business in MI (2E)	$16.95
		MINNESOTA TITLES	
_____	1-57248-142-0	How to File for Divorce in MN	$21.95

Qty	ISBN	Title	Ret
		NEW YORK TITLES	
_____	1-57248-141-2	How to File for Divorce in NY (2E)	$2
_____	1-57248-105-6	How to Form a Corporation in NY	$2
_____	1-57248-095-5	How to Make a NY Will (2E)	$1
_____	1-57071-185-2	How to Start a Business in NY	$1
_____	1-57071-187-9	How to Win in Small Claims Court in NY	$1
_____	1-57071-186-0	Landlords' Rights and Duties in NY	$2
_____	1-57071-188-7	New York Power of Attorney Handbook	$1
_____	1-57248-122-6	Tenants' Rights in NY	$2
		NORTH CAROLINA TITLES	
_____	1-57071-326-X	How to File for Divorce in NC (2E)	$2
_____	1-57248-129-3	How to Make a NC Will (3E)	$1
_____	1-57248-096-3	How to Start a Business in NC (2E)	$1
_____	1-57248-091-2	Landlords' Rights & Duties in NC	$2
		OHIO TITLES	
_____	1-57248-190-0	How to File for Divorce in OH (2E)	$2
		PENNSYLVANIA TITLES	
_____	1-57248-127-7	How to File for Divorce in PA (2E)	$2
_____	1-57248-094-7	How to Make a PA Will (2E)	$1
_____	1-57248-112-9	How to Start a Business in PA (2E)	$18
_____	1-57071-179-8	Landlords' Rights and Duties in PA	$19
		TEXAS TITLES	
_____	1-57071-330-8	How to File for Divorce in TX (2E)	$21
_____	1-57248-114-5	How to Form a Corporation in TX (2E)	$24
_____	1-57071-417-7	How to Make a TX Will (2E)	$16
_____	1-57071-418-5	How to Probate an Estate in TX (2E)	$22
_____	1-57071-365-0	How to Start a Business in TX (2E)	$18
_____	1-57248-111-0	How to Win in Small Claims Court in TX (2E)	$16
_____	1-57248-110-2	Landlords' Rights and Duties in TX (2E)	$21

SUBTOTAL THIS PAGE _____

SUBTOTAL PREVIOUS PAGE _____

Illinois residents add 6.75% sales tax _____

Connecticut residents add 6% state sales tax _____

Shipping — $5.00 for 1st book, $1.00 each additional _____

TOTAL _____